O9-BTJ-361

THE TREATIES OF 1778

INSTITUT FRANÇAIS DE WASHINGTON

EXTRACT FROM THE ACT OF INCORPORATION

"An association *to promote* in the United States of America the study of French civilization and history, literature and art, and *to preserve* the memory of French contributions to the development of American civilization *by endowing* or otherwise aiding in the establishment of Professorships, Courses of Lectures, Fellowships, and Scholarships, prizes and awards, libraries, archives and museums, in cooperation with Universities, Colleges, Learned Societies or Individuals, and *by publishing* documents, special studies and periodicals."

The certificate of incorporation was filed at Washington, D. C., on the 23rd day of December, 1926, the one hundred and fiftieth anniversary of the day when Benjamin Franklin arrived in Paris to negotiate a Treaty of Amity and Commerce between the United States of America and France.

HISTORICAL DOCUMENTS
INSTITUT FRANÇAIS DE WASHINGTON

CAHIER I

THE TREATIES OF 1778

AND ALLIED DOCUMENTS

EDITED BY G. CHINARD

WITH
AN INTRODUCTION
BY

JAMES BROWN SCOTT

THE JOHNS HOPKINS PRESS
BALTIMORE
1928

The Lord Baltimore Press
BALTIMORE, MD., U. S. A.

INTRODUCTION.

On February 6th of this year of 1928, it will be exactly one hundred and fifty years since M. Gérard, on behalf of Louis XVI, the young and inexperienced King of France, and Benjamin Franklin, Silas Deane, and Arthur Lee, on behalf of the thirteen English-speaking colonies in North America, which had declared their independence of Great Britain on July 4, 1776, put their seals and signatures to an epoch-making document.

In fact, two treaties were signed on the same day: one of alliance, and one of amity and commerce, the negotiation of which, upon terms of equality with France, recognized, because of the negotiation, the independence of the colonies, called for the first time in the Declaration of Independence, "the United States of America."

There is recognition and recognition—just and permissible recognition in international law, when the action is the acknowledgment of an existing fact; and recognition as a fact of what is, in reality, not so—an action condemned by the law of nations, although occasionally found in its practice. The thirteen States were at the time united by outward oppression, but not in law, as the Articles of Confederation creating a legal union had not been ratified by all the States, and therefore were not effective until March 1, 1781, when Maryland, the last of the thirteen joined the Confederation.

The High Contracting Parties knew what they were doing. It was, of course, in the interest of the United States that their independence should be acknowledged; it was assuredly not in the interest of either that matters should stop there, as the recognition under the Treaty of Amity and Commerce would not of itself change the fact that the States were struggling to obtain what they had not yet acquired: independence of Great Britain. It was thought by the government of France to be in its interest to have the United States separated once and for all from Great Britain, in order to redress the balance of power in Europe, which had been destroyed by the conquest of Canada by Great Britain through the Seven Years' War, and its possession confirmed by the Treaty of Paris of February 10, 1763,[1] which had, roughly speaking, bounded the possessions of the two countries by the Mississippi.

[1] De Martens, *Recueil de Traités* (2d edition, 1817), Tome I, p. 104.

Canada had remained loyal to Great Britain upon the outbreak of the American Revolution although the United States had sought to bring it into the conflict with the mother-country. The Floridas, East and West, which had passed from Spain to Great Britain by the Treaty of Paris of 1763, likewise remained loyal. The cession to Spain of Louisiana, lying west of the Mississippi and protruding as it were a trifle to the east near its mouth, therefore confined the colonies recognized by France as the United States to the territory situated between Canada and the Floridas to the east of Louisiana, then a newly acquired Spanish possession. The contest, however, was one for the possession of an empire. To render its acquisition by the United States certain, and to redress the balance of power in the interest of France, a military alliance placing at the disposal of the United States the money, the army and the navy of that Power was necessary. The alliance was concluded on the ever-memorable day of February 6, 1778, by plenipotentiaries on behalf of the two countries. Both knew that it was the complement of the Treaty of Amity and Commerce; indeed, the American plan for a treaty with a European Power included both. That European Power—France—preferred them separate, and separate they were.

The purpose of the "*Cahier*" which the Institut Français de Washington publishes in this, its first appearance before the public, is, by means of the original texts of carefully chosen documents, to make clear the origin, nature, and result of the collaboration of the United States and France, through which our commercial equality with France was recognized and assured in the Treaty of Amity and Commerce, and our independence procured through the participation of France in the war of the American Revolution.

* * *

France had long meditated the action which it ultimately took on February 6, 1778. It had greatly suffered by the Seven Years' War, which had made of the island kingdom across the Channel the most powerful country in the world. The policy of France was to prepare itself for the day when the victor and the vanquished in the Seven Years' War should find themselves again at war. Spain, as an ally of France, was compensated by that country for its losses by the cession of Louisiana. A secret agreement known as the "Family Compact" [1] bound the

[1] August 15, 1761. De Martens, *Recueil,* Tome I, p. 16.

sovereigns of the two countries, both members of the House of Bourbon, to join their forces against the common enemy when the day of trial should come.

France needed a navy strong enough to prevent the seizure of its vessels before the outbreak of hostilities and after the war had officially begun, in order to defend itself successfully on land and sea against its enemy. Therefore steps were taken to put the French fleets upon a footing of equality with those of Great Britain, and it was to be through the participation of Spain in the forthcoming war that their combined fleets should command the seas. Hence it was that France was anxious to have Spain declare war at the same time with it against Great Britain. The interests of the two Powers, however, while the same in so far as Great Britain was concerned, were vastly different. France was willing to renounce the reacquisition of Canada as the result of a successful war. Spain was unwilling to lose possession of its American colonies through an unsuccessful war and properly hesitated, by going to war on the pretext of securing the independence of the United States, to furnish its own possessions in America a precedent for revolt against their mother-country. However, an "Act Separate and Secret" was concluded by the plenipotentiaries of France and of the United States at one and the same time with the treaties reserving expressly, "to his said Catholick Majesty, the Power of acceding to the said Treaties, and to participate in their stipulations at such time as he shall judge proper." [1]

Eventually Spain bound itself by the Treaty of Aranjuez, of April 12, 1779, to join the war against Great Britain, and it entered as the ally of France in July of that year. The united fleets of France and Spain gave to France and its ally, the United States (for Spain did not enter into an alliance with the United States), the command of the seas at a critical moment. The appearance of a French fleet under Admiral de Grasse at Yorktown in 1781 forced the capitulation of a second British army, with the first surrender of a British fleet and, as it turned out, secured the independence of the United States, which had been declared by the Treaty of Alliance to be the sole purpose of its negotiation.

The colonies had been willing to make concessions to Spain in the hope of securing its aid, but although unwilling to ally itself with the States, lest revolution should have an added precedent, its aid should

[1] *Journals of the Continental Congress,* 1774-1789. (Library of Congress edition), Vol. XI, 1778, p. 454.

never be overlooked nor forgotten. For did not the great Washington himself say, in the dark days of 1778, after Valley Forge, during which the treaty with France was concluded: "If the Spaniards would but join their Fleets to those of France, & commence hostilities, my doubts would all subside—without it, I fear, the British Navy has it too much in its power to counteract the Schemes of France." [1]

*

* *

France might have concluded one or the other treaty any time after the Declaration of Independence, or indeed before that, had it so desired. Public sentiment was in favor of the colonies. But the defeat of Long Island (August 27, 1776) caused the French Government to hold off. There was, however, a fear that the colonies might fail, which caused France to venture to support them, lest they should fall into the power of Great Britain. However, the capitulation of a British army at Saratoga on the 17th day of October, 1777, with the indirect aid of France, offered the prospect of the capitulation of a second British army and fleet with the direct aid of France. This happened at Yorktown, October 19, 1781.

The victory of Saratoga had come at a moment of great depression. Washington with a freezing, dwindling, and starving army was in winter quarters at Valley Forge. The Major General commanding the northern army, one Horatio Gates by name, appropriated the initiative and the abilities of others, and, wreathed with the laurels to which he had no claim, lost his head and aspired to displace Washington as Commander-in-Chief, which, as we were later to know, would have been well-nigh the greatest misfortune that could have befallen American arms. Washington's credit was at its lowest. A British army under Sir William Howe occupied Philadelphia. The attack upon Germantown (October 4, 1777) had failed, and the American cause seemed to many to be in a bad way. Curiously enough the French appeared to be much impressed by the "staying" qualities of the Americans, who could stand a rebuff like Germantown and face the enemy.

However, the capitulation of the British army at Saratoga was such an overwhelming success that on October 31, 1777, the Continental Congress appointed a Committee of Three "to prepare a recommenda-

[1] George Washington to Gouverneur Morris, October 4, 1778. Autographed draft signed G. W. The Papers of George Washington, Vol. 86; 1778. Sept. 28–Oct. 4 (Library of Congress, 1915), p. 11347.

tion to the several states, to set apart a day of thanksgiving, for the signal success, lately obtained over the enemies of these United States." [1] Of this committee, Samuel Adams was chairman, and the report, in his handwriting, was, with a trifling modification of style, adopted November 1, 1777. The day set, the 18th of December, said to be the first "Continental thanksgiving day" [2] was indeed one of thanksgiving to three anxious representatives of the United States in France, as well as to their countrymen at home; for it was on the 18th that they wrote their communication to the Continental Congress, stating that the day before, M. Gérard, representing the Minister of Foreign Affairs, had waited upon them at Passy, to inform them that his Royal Master had decided to recognize their independence and to conclude a treaty of amity and commerce, and also one of alliance in case war should be the outcome of recognition.

Spain stood in the way of an immediate treaty, as France wished to secure that country as an ally before taking the final step. But on January 30, 1778, the King of France granted to M. Gérard—who had stated his Majesty's intention to the American Commissioners on December 17, 1777—full powers to conclude the treaties upon the terms stated in the Commissioners' communication of December 18th. This day, and especially that of February 6th, had long been awaited by the American Commissioners.

*
* *

As far back as November 29, 1775, the Continental Congress had appointed a Committee of Correspondence of five members, to get and to keep in touch with "our friends in Great Britain, Ireland, and other parts of the world." [3] This antedated the Declaration of Independence by several months.

It appeared to the Committee that the Continental Congress should have an agent, preferably one of its members, in France, in order to "sound out" its government, to learn the terms upon which the acknowledgment of their independence might be obtained, and the ways and means by which that event might be facilitated. Silas Deane, then a Delegate from Connecticut, was selected, in an evil hour for himself, and yet to the advantage of the United States on many occasions.

[1] *Journals,* IX: 851.

[2] W. De Loss Love, *The Fasts and Thanksgiving Days of New England* (1895), p. 400.

[3] *Journals,* III: 392.

The letter of instructions, dated March 3, 1776, proceeded from the deft hand of Benjamin Franklin, himself soon to represent the United States in France as his country has never, before or since, been represented in any part of the world.[1]

Deane was to go to France as a merchant engaged "in the business of providing goods for the Indian trade," as it was probable that France would not like "it should be known publicly that any agent from the Colonies" was in that country. His "business" was to appear to the French what it often is today, "the gratifying of that curiosity, which draws numbers thither yearly, merely to see so famous a city." His "curiosity" was to be greater for M. de Vergennes, who was then and until the Revolution and the day of his death, Minister of Foreign Affairs.

Mr. Deane was to ask for an audience, in which he should communicate "something" which might be "mutually beneficial to France and the North American Colonies." At the audience he was to show his letter of credit, stating, among other things, that he was seeking arms and munitions necessary for the defense of his country against Great Britain; "that France," so the letter ran, "had been pitched on for the first application," as "France would be looked upon as the power whose friendship it would be fittest for us to obtain and cultivate." Commercial advantages were to be dangled before the eyes of the Minister, with the assurance that the trade would be "extremely valuable" after the independence of the United States. At the present time he was to be informed that they wanted "clothing and arms for twenty-five thousand men, with a suitable quantity of ammunition, and one hundred field pieces," in addition to "great quantities of linens and woolens, with other articles for the Indian trade, which you are now actually purchasing, and for which you ask no credit, and that the whole, if France should grant the other supplies, would make a cargo which it might be well to secure by a convoy of two or three ships of war."

It was foreseen that M. de Vergennes might be reserved in his manner and cautious in expression. If so, Mr. Deane was to shorten his visit, but to say that he would be glad to wait upon His Excellency the Minister of Foreign Affairs at some future time, if that should be the Minister's pleasure. If at a future conference M. de Vergennes should "be more free, and you find a disposition to favor the Colonies" Deane

[1] *Revolutionary Diplomatic Correspondence of the United States,* edited by Francis Wharton, Vol. II (1889), p. 78.

was instructed to "acquaint him that they must necessarily be anxious to know the disposition of France on certain points, ... such as whether, if the Colonies should be forced to form themselves into an independent State, France would probably acknowledge them as such, receive their embassadors, enter into any treaty or alliance with them, for commerce or defense, or both? If so, on what principal conditions?"

Deane was further to inform him that he was soon to communicate with the Continental Congress, and that the Minister could rely upon his "fidelity and secrecy in transmitting carefully anything he would wish to convey to the Congress on that subject."

These instructions were likewise before the Declaration of Independence.

The American cause was advanced in various ways, partly through Arthur Lee, who had been Franklin's successor as agent of Massachusetts in London, more largely through Deane himself, and above all, through Beaumarchais, in a series of intrigues as clever as anything he wrote in the *Barbier de Séville* or the *Mariage de Figaro,* and infinitely more interesting to the good people of the United States of that day; and finally through Benjamin Franklin, who, on September 26, 1776, was designated to repair to Paris to reinforce Deane and Lee.

The Commission to Paris had appeared too important for a single person. Therefore, it was decided to appoint three Commissioners, and on September 26, 1776, Benjamin Franklin, Silas Deane and Thomas Jefferson were selected. Jefferson declining, Arthur Lee was appointed in his stead.

The Commissioners were to enter into negotiations with the Government of France, and therefore it became necessary to furnish them with credentials. A Committee was appointed immediately upon the selection of the Commissioners. Two days later, letters of credence were prepared and adopted, to enable the Commissioners to negotiate a treaty of commerce with France.

The instructions to proposed Commissioners had been adopted four days previously. As this is the first occasion on which the United States furnished its agents with letters of credence—the instructions had been prepared four days earlier—the text of this short but important document is given in full:[1]

The delegates of the United States of New Hampshire, Massachusetts Bay, Rhode Island, Connecticut, New York, New Jersey, Pennsylvania,

[1] Journals, V: 833.

Delaware, Maryland, Virginia, North Carolina, South Carolina, and Georgia, to all who shall see these presents, send greeting.

Whereas a trade upon equal terms between the subjects of his most christian majesty the king of France, and the people of these states, will be beneficial to both nations—Know ye therefore, that we, confiding in the prudence and integrity of [here were inserted the names of Franklin, Deane and Lee] have appointed and deputed, and by these presents do appoint and depute them the said [names] our commissioners, giving and granting to them the said [names] or any two of them, and in case of death, absence, or disability of any two, to any one of them, full power to communicate, treat, agree and conclude with his most christian majesty, the king of France, or with such person or persons as shall by him be for that purpose authorized, of and upon a true and sincere friendship, and a firm, inviolable, and universal peace, for the defence, protection and safety of the navigation and mutual commerce of the subjects of his most christian majesty and the people of the United States; and to do all other things, which may conduce to those desirable ends; and promising in good faith to ratify whatsoever our said commissioners shall transact in the premises.

Done in Congress, at Philadelphia, the thirtieth day of September, in the year of our Lord, one thousand seven hundred and seventy six. In testimony whereof, the President, by order of the said Congress, hath hereunto subscribed his name, and affixed his seal.

Dr. Franklin sailed from Philadelphia aboard the *Reprisal,* a small Federal vessel, which, leaving Delaware Bay on the 29th of October, arrived thirty days later in Quiberon Bay. " Our voyage," he said in a letter to John Hancock, written from Nantes, December 8, 1776, " though not long, was rough, and I feel myself weakened by it; but I now recover strength daily, and in a few days shall be able to undertake the journey to Paris." [1] He arrived there on the 22nd. On the 23rd, the three Commissioners asked an audience with His Excellency the Minister of Foreign Affairs. It was granted on the 28th, and the negotiations, although informal, were begun which were ultimately to terminate in the treaties of amity and commerce and alliance of February 6, 1778.

A communication from Messrs. Franklin and Deane stated that the Treaties would be sent by special vessel. It was the frigate *Sensible,* carrying Simeon Deane, brother of Silas, with the precious papers. It arrived at Falmouth (Portland), in Casco Bay, on April 13th, after a passage of thirty-five days. Deane reached York town on May 2nd, the very day on which the Continental Congress had "Adjourned to 10 o'clock on Monday," [2] unaware of the " tidings of great joy " which

[1] Smyth: VI; 474.
[2] Journals, XI, 417.

were to reach the President in the afternoon. An additional entry of the Journal for May 2nd stated it all:

During the adjournment, Mr. [Simeon] Deane, brother to S[ilas] Deane, Esqr. one of the commissioners at the court of Versailles, arrived express from France, with sundry important despatches; Whereupon,

Congress was convened, and the despatches laid before them. Among which a treaty of commerce and alliance, concluded between the king of France and the United States of America, on the 6 February last.

On Monday, the 4th of May, Congress "took into consideration the treaties . . . . and after some time spent thereon, adjourned to 3 o'clock."[1] In the afternoon there are several entries which, however formal and rigid in style, nevertheless allow the most casual reader to picture the scene and the all-pervading joy of the occasion:[2]

Congress resumed the consideration of the treaty of amity and commerce concluded at Paris, on the 6th of February, [here follow the names of the High Contracting Parties and the plenipotentiaries], and the same being read, duly weighed and considered,

Resolved unanimously, That the same be and is hereby ratified.

Congress also took into consideration the treaty of Alliance, concluded at Paris on the 6 day of February, 1778, [here follow the names of the High Contracting Parties and the plenipotentiaries], and the same being read, duly weighed and considered.

Resolved, unanimously, That the same be and is hereby ratified.

Congress also took into consideration an "Act separate and secret," [the proposed treaty with Spain], concluded at Paris, the 6 day of February, 1778, [here follow the names of the High Contracting Parties], signed as the above, and the same being duly weighed,

Resolved, unanimously, That the same be, and is hereby ratified.

There is, however, one of a different character:

Resolved, That this Congress entertain the highest sense of the magnanimity and wisdom of his most Christian majesty, so strongly exemplified in the treaty of amity and commerce, and the treaty of alliance, ... and the commissioners, or any of them, representing these States at the court of France, are directed to present the grateful acknowledgments of this Congress to his most Christian majesty, for his truly magnanimous conduct respecting these states, in the said generous and disinterested treaties, and to assure his majesty, on the part of this Congress, it is sincerely wished that the friendship so happily commenced between France and these United States may be perpetual.[3]

[1] *Ibid.*, p. 419.

[2] *Ibid.*, p. 457.

[3] *Ibid.*, pp. 457-458.

The Treaty of Amity and Commerce with France was the first treaty which these United States concluded with any Power, and the Treaty of Alliance is the first and only treaty of alliance concluded by the United States with any Power. The friendship so happily begun still continues.

Two matters still confronted the Continental Congress. One was the form of ratification, for which purpose, on May 4th, at the very end of the session, a committee of three was appointed "to prepare the form of ratification of the foregoing treaties." No time was lost. On the following day, the form was prepared, read and agreed to. It is the first act of ratification which these United States had ever prepared.

The second matter was "to prepare a proper publication on the present occasion." [1]

On May 6th, the committee to which the draft for publication had been recommended, brought in a draft which had the good fortune to be approved. Unmindful of, or perhaps unfamiliar with the diplomatic proprieties required by the occasion, the Continental Congress appears to have made known the terms of the treaties without the authorization of His Most Christian Majesty. However, they were not to be blamed for this, because the ink was hardly dry before the terms of the treaties were in the possession of the British Government, and before the arrival of the treaties in America the British and French Ambassadors had been withdrawn by their respective governments, and the two countries were at war.

For present purposes the matter of interest is the terms in which the treaties were made known to the American people:

> It is recommended to the Inhabitants of these United States, that they regard and treat the subjects of France as those of a magnanimous and generous Ally. For it is with pleasure that Congress inform the Public that his most Christian Majesty, declining to avail himself of the situation of these United States, engaged in a war with a powerful and cruel Enemy, hath with a magnamity becoming a great Prince, generously treated on terms of perfect equality and mutual benefit. And to the end that all proper alacrity may be shewn in giving aid and protection to the commerce, property and persons, of the subjects of his Most Christian Majesty, the following extracts from said Treaties are published for the information of all, and for regulating the conduct of those whom it may more immediately concern.[2]

[1] *Ibid.*, p. 464.
[2] *Ibid.*, p. 468.

In another part of the resolution adopted the same day, the King of France is declared to have rendered himself " the protector of the rights of mankind."

On November 4th the Continental Congress:

Ordered, That 300 copies of the treaties of amity and commerce, and of alliance, entered into between his most Christian majesty and the United States of America, be printed.

They were printed by John Dunlap, in Philadelphia, as their negotiation had caused its evacuation by the British army under Sir Henry Clinton on June 18, 1778. He was followed on his retreat to New York by Washington's army from Valley Forge and beaten at Monmouth, in the State of New Jersey, on June 28, 1778.

*
* *

The young Republic of the west had persuaded the oldest monarchy in Europe to make common cause with it, although as it later turned out, the French Revolution, the outcome of the American, was to take the life of the King, overturning the old régime and replacing it with a Republic without, however, having the republican traditions necessary to make the new form of government a success.

On June 7, 1776, it was by the Continental Congress

Resolved, That these United Colonies are, and of right ought to be, free and independent States, that they are absolved from all allegiance to the British Crown, and that all political connection between them and the State of Great Britain is, and ought to be, totally dissolved.

That it is expedient forthwith to take the most effectual measures for forming foreign Alliances.

That a plan of confederation be prepared and transmitted to the respective Colonies for their consideration and approbation.[1]

The first of these resolutions formed the basis of the resolution of independence adopted on the 2nd of July, and the declaration of two days later. The plan of confederation eventually assumed the form and shape of the Articles of Confederation adopted by the Congress on November 15, 1777, and ratified by the last of the thirteen States on March 1, 1781.

The second resolution is the one of present interest. On June 11, 1776, a Committee was appointed " to prepare a plan of treaties to be proposed to foreign powers." On the next day a committee of five was appointed, consisting of John Dickinson, Benjamin Franklin, John

[1] *Journals,* V: 425.

Adams, Benjamin Harrison, and Robert Morris. On the 18th of July, two weeks after the proclamation of the Declaration of Independence, the Committee brought in a plan of treaties, the original draft of which is in the handwriting of John Adams.[1]

It consisted of some thirty articles dealing with amity and commerce, and above and beyond all, in Articles 7, 8, 9, and 10, with the burning question of an alliance.

The proposed treaty was to be between "the most serene and mighty Prince, Lewis the Sixteenth, the most Christian King, his Heirs and Successors, and the united States of America." In the original draft neither the King nor the United States were mentioned by name, the first paragraph of the Treaty reading:

> There Shall be a firm, inviolable, and universal peace, and a true and Sincere friendship between A. and B. and the Subjects of A. and of B. and between the Countries, Islands, Cities and towns Situate under the Jurisdiction of A. and of B. and the people and inhabitants thereof of every degree, without exception of persons or places; and the Terms herein after Mentioned Shall be perpetual between A. and B.[2]

The men of the day were looking out for the future, a future most clearly evidenced by Article 8, which deserves quotation. In its original form, before "the most Christian King and the King of Great Britain" had replaced letters of the alphabet, it read:

> In Case of any War between A. and ——, A. Shall never invade, nor attempt to invade or get possession for himself of ——, nor any of the Countries Cities or towns on the Continent of ——, nor of the Islands of ——, nor any other Island lying near to the Continent, in the Seas, or in any Gulph, bay or river thereof, it being the true intent and Meaning of this Treaty, that the Said B. Shall have the Sole, exclusive, undivided and perpetual possession of all the Countries, Cities and towns on the Said Continent, and of all Islands near to it, whenever they Shall be confederated or United with B. That A. Shall retain the Same rights of Fishing on the Banks of Newfoundland and all other Rights relating to any of the Said Islands which She is entitled to by virtue of the Treaty of Paris.[3]

The man whose hand drafted that article was in favor of the Monroe Doctrine when it was proclaimed in 1823; and it is interesting to note that his son, John Quincy Adams, was Secretary of State to President Monroe, whose name the doctrine bears, although the son of the original advocate of the doctrine was himself largely responsible for it. A year

[1] *Ibid.*, p. 576, note 1.
[2] Force Transcript 47, No. 161, p. 199, in the Library of Congress, Washington, D. C.
[3] *Ibid.*, pp. 202-203.

before the draft, John Adams had said that as a Treaty of Alliance would "entangle us in any future wars in Europe; . . . . we ought to lay it down, as a first principle and a maxim never to be forgotten, to maintain an entire neutrality in all future European wars." [1] Later, after the "questionable" Treaty of Alliance had resulted in the independence of these United States, the same John Adams has an entry in his diary of November 18, 1782,[2] which is to the same effect, and more outspoken:

"You are afraid," says Mr. Oswald [3] to-day, "of being made the tools of the powers of Europe." "Indeed I am," says I. "What powers?" said he. "All of them," said I. "It is obvious that all the powers of Europe will be continually manoeuvring with us, to work us into their real or imaginary balances of power. They will all wish to make of us a make-weight candle, when they are weighing out their pounds. Indeed, it is not surprising; for we shall very often, if not always, be able to turn the scale. But I think it ought to be our rule not to meddle; and that of all the powers of Europe, not to desire us, or, perhaps, even to permit us, to interfere, if they can help it."

It is evident from the language of Article 8 and the expression "Continent," that America was to be for the Americans.

John Adams's draft was read, considered, and slightly amended, principally by the omission here and there of a phrase. It was not adopted at the time, but "*Ordered,* To lie on the table."

The plan of a treaty came up again on September 17th, and was adopted. It was, of course, to be accompanied by instructions. Their discussion was adjourned to the morrow, and a further consideration of them postponed on that day. On September 24th the Congress took up the instructions and "debated by paragraphs, and amended," they were agreed to.[4]

The Congress and the American agents were ready to negotiate, and to sign a treaty or treaties as close to the instructions as possible, and in any event to get the treaties even though they should differ from the instructions, which after all were to guide not to control the negotiators.

The great day came at last—the 6th of February, 1778—when the Treaty of Amity and Commerce, and above and beyond all, the Treaty

[1] *The Works of John Adams,* by Charles Francis Adams, Vol. II, Autobiography (1850), p. 505.

[2] *Ibid.,* Vol. III (1851), p. 316.

[3] British negotiator of the Peace Treaty with Great Britain.

[4] *Journals,* V: 813.

of Alliance, separate and distinct from it, were signed. The sole purpose of the latter was the independence of the United States:

> The essential and direct end [so Article 2 reads] of the present defensive alliance is, to maintain effectually the liberty, sovereignty, and independence absolute and unlimited of the said United States, as well in matters of government as of commerce.

Article 8 of the Congressional plan appears in modified form in Articles 5, 6 and 7, to the effect that France was not to attempt to reconquer its continental possessions which had passed to Great Britain by the Treaty of Paris of 1763; if conquered by the allies, they were to pass to the United States. On the other hand, British islands situated in the Gulf of Mexico, or near that Gulf were, if conquered, to pass to the Crown of France.

The spirit of the treaties is as remarkable as the letter. History affords few, if any examples of such frankness, straightforwardness and generosity of a great Power to a weak and struggling ally. The States were, according to M. Gérard's instructions, to be treated upon a footing of equality, with no advantage to be taken of their present weakness, to the end that when grown strong and great, the treaties would be approved by the two High Contracting Parties.

M. Gérard admitted frankly, as reported by the American Commissioners,[1] that besides the King's "real Goodwill to us and our Cause, it was manifestly the Interest of France that the Power of England should be diminished by our Separation from it." The Most Christian King imposed but a single condition: that "we in no Peace to be made with England should give up our Independency, and return to the Obedience of that Government," leaving the United States free to conclude a treaty with Great Britain upon those terms, separately or conjointly as it should choose, with France.

These principles appear in a modified form in Article 8 of the Treaty of Alliance:

> Neither of the two Parties shall conclude either Truce or Peace with Great Britain, without the formal consent of the other first obtain'd; and they mutually engage not to lay down their arms until the Independence of the united States shall have been formally, or tacitly, assured by the Treaty or Treaties, that shall terminate the War.

Under date of February 8, 1778, Franklin and Deane informed the President of the Continental Congress that the treaties had been con-

[1] Franklin, Deane, and Lee to the Committee of Foreign Affairs, Passy, December 18, 1777. From triplicate of original in the Library of Congress.

cluded, and after a brief summary of their terms, said: "you will soon have the whole by a safer Conveyance, a Frigate being appointed to carry our Dispatches." The frigate, appropriately named the *Sensible* "carried" Simeon Deane, brother of Silas, and its more precious cargo, the treaties. "We only observe to you, and with Pleasure, that we have found thro'out this Business the greatest Cordiality in this Court; and that no Advantage has been taken or attempted to be taken of our present Difficulties to obtain hard Terms from us; but such has been the King's Magnanimity & Goodness, that he has proposed none which we might not readily have agreed to in a State of full Prosperity & established Power. The principle laid down as the Basis of the Treaty being as declared in the Preamble, 'the most perfect Equality and Reciprocity' the Privileges in Trade, &c. are mutual, and none are given to France, but what we are at Liberty to grant to any other Nation." [1]

This is indeed true, but it is not the whole truth. Article 8 of the Treaty provides that France would accord to the United States several free ports. The exact situation is stated with great clearness and brevity, in a French work of authority:

> Article 8 of the Treaty of Commerce of 1778 between France and the United States stipulated that France should grant several free ports to the Republic. Vergennes thought of designating Bayonne, where there was less to be feared from contraband, on the very score of the privileges of the port. But the customs rights had to be redeemed from the *Ferme générale* and from the house of Grammont. . . . Vergennes likewise opened the port of Lorient to the United States.[2]

This appears to be the first instance in which the exclusive commercial system of France was changed in order to meet the desires of their good friends the Americans.

On May 4, 1778, Congress had ratified the Treaties of Amity and Commerce, and Alliance, and the Secret Treaty, but its members doubted the advisability of Articles 11 and 12 of the first. Therefore, on May 5, 1778, it was "*Resolved,* That the commissioners, or any one of them, representing these states at the court of France, be instructed to inform that court that, although Congress have readily ratified the treaties of amity and commerce, and treaty of alliance, and the act, separate and

[1] Papers of the Continental Congress. Letters of the Joint Commissioners. V. 85, pp. 113-114.

[2] G. Schelle, *Du Pont de Nemours et l'École Physiocratique,* Paris (1888), p. 217, n. 221.

secret, between his most Christian majesty and these United States, in order to evince more clearly their sense of the magnanimity and goodness of his most Christian majesty, evidenced in the said treaties; yet, from a sincere desire of rendering the friendship and alliance, so happily begun, permanent and perpetual, and being apprehensive that differences may arise from the 11 and 12 articles in the treaty of amity and commerce, Congress are desirous that the said 11 and 12 articles may be revoked and utterly expunged."[1] The Commissioners were therefore instructed, "to use their best endeavours to procure the abolition of the said 11 and 12 articles of the said treaty."

By the 11th Article it was agreed that there should never be any export tax upon molasses taken by subjects of the United States "from the islands of America, which belong, or may hereafter appertain, to his most christian majesty."[2] Article 12, on the other hand, inasmuch as the life and breath of the Treaty of Amity and Commerce was to be and actually was "the most perfect equality and reciprocity" between the High Contracting Parties, provided that no export tax was to be levied by the United States upon "any kind of merchandise" which the subjects of His Most Christian Majesty should "take from the countries and possessions present or future of any of the thirteen United States, for the use of the islands which shall furnish molasses."[3] Molasses, it may be said in passing, has played a great rôle in the American world, and those at all familiar with the colonial history of the United States appreciate its importance, especially to the New England colonies, one of whose staples was "rum." Indeed, it is not too much to say that the "molasses question" was one of the causes of the Revolution.

With the request on the part of the three American Commissioners, His Most Christian Majesty graciously complied, on September 1, 1778.

*

* *

There are some observations of a rather technical kind which may be made in regard to the treaties. They are in French and English, and signed by the representatives of both Contracting Parties. The original was in French, as is stated in the final paragraph of each treaty. This was a gracious concession on the part of the great ally, whose language was that of the diplomatic as well as of the social world, and could, indeed, lay claim to a universal character and a universal usage.

[1] *Journals,* XI: 459-460.

[2] *Ibid.,* p. 428.

[3] *Ibid.,* pp. 428-429.

Professor Chinard, interested in all things American as well as French, says:

I have closely examined the translation: it is remarkable. For certain of the articles, nevertheless, the thing is rather amusing. On the whole the original text, or draft treaty, was in English. This English was translated into French to be discussed; then, in several cases, re-translated into the original language when the definitive translation of the treaty was made. As on both sides the matter was dealt with by people who knew how to handle their language, the two texts are of rare quality.

In this case and through simple courtesy to a nation which was new and consequently understood but imperfectly the diplomatic language of Europe, France in signing could even make a few concessions. But doubtless this is not the place to discuss such a matter.[1]

The two treaties were signed on February 6, 1778; they were ratified by the Continental Congress on May 4, 1778; they were ratified by France July 16, 1778.

The question is often asked, and sometimes arises in practice, as to the date at which a treaty goes into effect. The intention of the parties decides the matter. When they fix a date at which the treaty shall become operative, it speaks from that date. If, however, the High Contracting Parties have not expressly determined the matter, their intention may be presumed from the usage and customs of nations. Originally the sovereign was reputed to make the treaty through his representative specially authorized by what are called in the language of diplomacy "full powers." The treaty in such case would speak from the date of his signature. In the course of time, however, the full power came to be looked upon as an authority to negotiate, with the right reserved to the sovereign to approve the use which his representative had made of the full power. This was a check upon indiscreet or questionable conduct on the part of the agent, and, although delaying the treaty, was in the interest of good faith. During the eighteenth century it had become the custom to read into full powers the reservation of approval on the part of the negotiating Powers through the instrument of ratification.[2]

[1] Letter to Mr. Scott dated January 2, 1928.

[2] A great judge, Sir William Scott, later Lord Stowell, whose opinions are justly ranked among the masterpieces of international law, has put the law and the case in a few sentences:

"The question, therefore, comes to this, whether a ratification is or is not necessary to give effect and validity to a treaty signed by plenipotentiaries. Upon abstract principles we know that, either in public or private transactions, the acts of those who are vested with a plenary power are binding upon the principal. But, as this

The rule is, admitting that by the practice of nations ratification is necessary, the question arises, from what date, that of the signature, or that of ratification, is the treaty to speak? In the absence of agreement to the contrary, it would seem that in public matters between nations as such, the obligation of the treaty relates back to its signatures, as the High Contracting Parties are reputed to know the contents of the treaties and bind themselves from the date of signature. In the case of provisions of the treaty affecting private persons and private rights, the date of ratification is to be preferred, inasmuch as, unlike the Contracting Parties, they can not know the contents of the treaty until it has been ratified and its terms made public.[1]

*
* *

We would be justified in supposing, if we did not know the joy which the treaties occasioned the good men and true at Valley Forge, to whom, in this country, the destiny of America was committed.

Washington was in fact informed before Congress, of the arrival of the treaties, and from Valley Forge, under date of May 1, 1778, he wrote to Henry Laurens, the President of the Continental Congress: "With infinite pleasure, I beg leave to congratulate Congress on the very important & interesting advices brought by the Frigate *L' Sensible*. Gen[l] McDougal & Mr. Deane were so obliging, as to transmit me the outlines of the good tidings. As soon as Congress may think it expedient

---

rule was in many cases found to be attended with inconvenience, the later usage of states has been to require a ratification, although the treaty may have been signed by plenipotentiaries. According to the practice now prevailing, a subsequent ratification is essentially necessary; and a strong confirmation of the truth of this position is, that there is hardly a modern treaty in which it is not expressly so stipulated; and, therefore, it is now to be presumed, that the powers of plenipotentiaries are limited by the condition of a subsequent ratification. The ratification may be a form, but it is an essential form; for the instrument, in point of legal efficacy, is imperfect without it. I need not add, that a ratification by one power alone is insufficient; that, if necessary at all, it must be mutual; and that the treaty is incomplete till it has been reciprocally ratified." *The Eliza Ann*, High Court of Admiralty, 1813, *1 Dodson, 244, 248.*

[1] "It is undoubtedly true, as a principle of international law, that, as respects the rights of either government under it, a treaty is considered as concluded and binding from the date of its signature. In this regard the exchange of ratifications has a retroactive effect, confirming the treaty from its date. But a different rule prevails where the treaty operates on individual rights. The principle of relation does not apply to rights of this character, which were vested before the treaty was ratified. In so far as it affects them, it is not considered as concluded until there is an exchange of ratifications." Mr. Justice Davis delivering the opinion of the court in *Haver* v. *Yaker*, Supreme Court of the United States, 1869. *9 Wallace*, 32, 34.

I shall be happy to have an opportunity of announcing to the army with the usual ceremony, such parts of the intelligence as may be proper & sanctified by authority. I have mentioned the matter to such officers as I have seen, and I believe no event was ever received with a more heartfelt joy." [1]

Congress, on its part, lost no time in communicating the good news to Washington, as appears from his letter to the President of the Congress of May 4, 1778: "Last night at 11 O'clock I was honored with your despatches of the 3d. The Contents afford me the most sensible pleasure. Mr. Simeon Deane had informed me, by a line from Bethlehem, that he was the Bearer of the Articles of alliance &c. between France and the States.

I shall defer celebrating this happy event in a suitable manner, until I have liberty from Congress to announce it publickly. I will only say, that the army are anxious to manifest their joy upon the occasion." [2]

Washington, as Commander-in-Chief, issued from headquarters at Valley Forge, on Tuesday, May 5, 1778, the following General Orders for manœuvers for the morrow:

It having pleased the Almighty ruler of the Universe propitiously to defend the Cause of the United American-States and finally by raising us up a powerful Friend among the Princes of the Earth to establish our liberty and Independence upon lasting foundations, it becomes us to set apart a day for gratefully acknowledging the divine Goodness & celebrating the important Event which we owe to his benign Interposition.—

The several Brigaders are to be assembled for this Purpose at nine o'Clock tomorrow morning when their Chaplains will communicate the Intelligence contain'd in the Postscript to the Pennsylvania Gazette of the 2nd instant and offer up a thanksgiving and deliver a discourse suitable to the Occasion— At half after ten o'Clock a Cannon will be fired, which is to be a signal for the men to be under Arms—The Brigade Inspectors will then inspect their Dress and Arms, form the Battalions according to instructions given them and announce to the Commanding Officers of Brigades that the Battalions are formed: The Brigadiers or Commandants will then appoint the Field Officers to command the Battalions, after which each Battalion will be ordered to load and ground their Arms.

At half after eleven a second Cannon be fired as a signal for the march upon which the several Brigades will begin their march by wheeling to the right by Platoons & proceed by the nearest way to the left of their ground

[1] The papers of the Continental Congress. Letters of Washington, Library of Congress, 152, Vol. VI, pp. 1-209, at p. 2.

[2] The papers of the Continental Congress. Letters of Washington, Library of Congress, Vol. VI, pp. 1-209, at p. 9.

in the new Position; this will be pointed out by the Brigade Inspectors—A third signal will be given upon which there will be discharge of thirteen Cannon; When the thirteen has fired a runing fire of the Infantry will begin on the right of Woodford's and continue throughout the whole front line, it will then be taken on the left of the second line and continue to the right—Upon a signal given, the whole Army will *Huzza* "Long Live the King of France"—The Artillery then begins again and fires thirteen rounds, this will be succeded by a second general discharge of the Musquetry in a runing fire—Huzza!—"And long live the friendly European Powers"—Then the last discharge of thirteen Pieces of Artillery will be given, followed by a General Runing fire and Huzza! To the American States".—

There will be no Exercise in the morning and the guards of the day will not parade 'till after the Feu de joie is finished, when the Brigade Major will march them out to the Grand Parade:— The Adjutants then will tell off their Battalions into eight Platoons and the commanding officer will re-conduct them to their Camps marching by the left.—

Major General Lord Stirling will command on the right, the Marquis De la fayette on the left and Baron De Kalb the second line—Each Major General will conduct the first Brigade of his Command to its ground, the other Brigades will be conducted by their commanding officers in separate columns—The Posts of each Bridge will be pointed out by Baron De Steuben's Aids—Maj[r] Walker will attend Lord Stirling—Major De Eponsiere the Marquis De la Fayette and Captain Lanfant the Baron De Kalb—The line is to be formed with the Interval of a foot between the files—

Each man is to have a Gill of rum—The Quarter-Masters of the several Brigades are to apply to the Adjutant General for an order on the Commissary of Military stores for the number of blank Cartridges that may be wanted.—[1]

The celebration passed off to Washington's satisfaction, inasmuch as he issued on the 7th, the following General Order:

The Commander in Chief takes particular Pleasure in acquainting the Army that their Conduct yesterday afforded him the highest Satisfaction:—The Exactness and order with which their Movements were performed is a pleasing Evidence of the Progress they are making in Military Improvement, and an earnest of the pleasing Perfection to which they will shortly arrive,—with a Continuance of that laudable Zeal and Emulation which so happily prevails;— . . . . [2]

"The General" then presented "his thanks to Baron Steuben, and the Gentlemen acting under him."[3]

[1] Washington Manuscripts, Orderly book, 1778, Jan. 1-Dec. 31. Varick transcript in Library of Congress, Washington, D. C., pp. 185-188.

[2] Washington Manuscripts, Orderly Book, 1778. Library of Congress, Washington, D. C., pp. 189-193.

[3] *Ibid.*

It is sometimes given to one man in a few chosen words to bare the soul of his countrymen. This happened to Robert Morris, who, in a letter of May 9th, addressed to General Washington, voiced the feelings of his countrymen:

> When I congratulate Your Excell^y on the great good news lately received from France, you will not expect me to express my Feelings, was I in your Company My Countenance might then, but my pen cannot express them. Most sincerely do I give you joy. Our Independence is undoubtedly Secured, our Country must be Free.[1]

*
* *

February 6, 1778, marks not merely a date in the history of the United States, but in the development of the political liberty of mankind.

JAMES BROWN SCOTT.

WASHINGTON, *January, 1928.*

[1] The Papers of George Washington, 73; 1778, April 26-May 12. Library of Congress, Washington, D. C., 1915, p. 9601.

I
THE PRELIMINARIES

PLAN OF TREATIES

INSTRUCTIONS TO THE AGENT

Editor's note. The story of the Plan of Treaties will be found in the following excerpts from the Journals of the Continental Congress:

Wednesday, June 12, 1776.

Resolved, That the Committee to prepare a plan of treaties to be proposed to foreign powers, consist of five members:

The members chosen, Mr. [John] Dickinson, Mr. [Benjamin] Franklin, Mr. J[ohn] Adams, Mr. [Benjamin] Harrison, and Mr. R[obert] Morris.

Thursday, July 18, 1776.

The committee appointed to prepare a plan of treaties to be entered into with foreign states or kingdoms, brought in a report, which was read.

Ordered, To lie on the table.

Tuesday, August 27, 1776.

Resolved, That the plan of the treaties, with the amendments, be referred to the committee who brought in the [original] plan, in order to draw up instructions pursuant to the amendments made by the committee of the whole.

That two members be added to the Committee.

The members chosen Mr. R[ichard] Henry Lee and Mr. [James] Wilson.

Thursday, August 29, 1776.

Resolved, That the committee to whom the plan of treaties, as amended, was re-committed, be empowered to prepare such further instructions as to them shall seem proper, and make report thereof to Congress.

The first draft of the plan may be found under July 18, 1776 in the *Journals of Congress* (Library of Congress edition), vol. v, p. 576. The final form of the plan as it appears in the *Journals of Congress* under September 17 is the only one given here. The preamble however has been taken from a minute in the hand writing of Charles Thomson, headed *Passed in Congress 17 Septbr. 1776,* and recently discovered by Dr. J. C. Fitzpatrick among documents sent to the Manuscript Division of the Library of Congress from the Department of State. It was called to my attention by Miss E. S. Kite. In this minute the United States and the King are mentioned by names and not by the letters A and B as in the printed text.

Considerable use has been made of the *Journals of the Continental Congress,* edited by Mr. Worthington Chauncey Ford. Some of the notes have been reproduced: they are indicated by the initials W. C. F. The editor's indebtedness to the well-known scholarship of Mr. Ford is gratefully acknowledged here.

THE PRELIMINARIES.

PLAN OF TREATIES.

JOURNALS OF CONGRESS.

Tuesday, September 17, 1776.

Congress took into consideration the plan of treaties to be proposed to foreign nations, [with] the amendments proposed by the committee of the whole.

Resolved, That the following plan of a treaty be proposed to His Most Christian Majesty.

There shall be a firm inviolable and universal peace and a true and sincere friendship between the most serene and mighty Prince Lewis sixteenth the most Christian King his heirs and successors and the United States of America; and the subjects of the most Christian King and of the said states; and between the countries, islands cities and towns situate under the jurisdiction of the most Christian King and of the said united states and the people and inhabitants thereof of every degree; without exception of persons or places; and the terms herein mentioned shall be perpetual between the most Christian King, his heirs and successors & the United States.

Art. I. The Subjects of the most Christian King shall pay no other Duties or Imposts in the Ports, Havens, Roads, Countries, Islands, Cities, or Towns of the said united States or any of them, than the Natives thereof, or any Commercial Companies established by them or any of them, shall pay, but shall enjoy all other the Rights, Liberties, Priviledges, Immunities, and Exemptions in Trade, Navigation and Commerce in passing from one Part thereof to another, and in going to and from the same, from and to any Part of the World, which the said Natives, or Companies enjoy.

Art. II. The Subjects, People and Inhabitants of the said united States, and every of them, shall pay no other Duties, or Imposts in the Ports, Havens, Roads, Countries, Islands, Cities, or Towns of the most Christian King, than the Natives of such Countries, Islands, Cities, or Towns of France, or any commercial Companies established by the most Christian King shall pay, but shall enjoy all other the Rights, Liberties,

Priviledges, Immunities and Exemptions in Trade, Navigation and Commerce, in passing from one port [Part] thereof to another, and in going to and from the same, from and to any Part of the World, which the said Natives, or Companies enjoy.

Art. III. His most Christian Majesty shall retain the same Rights of Fishery on the Banks of Newfoundland, and all other Rights relating to any of the said Islands, which he is entitled to by virtue of the Treaty of Paris.

Art. IV. The most Christian King shall endeavour, by all the Means in his Power to protect and defend all Vessels, and the Effects belonging to the Subjects, People, or Inhabitants of the said united States, or any of them, being in his Ports, Havens, or Roads, or on the Seas, near to his Countries, Islands, Cities, or Towns, and to recover and to restore, to the right owners, their Agents or Attornies, all such Vessells, and Effects, which shall be taken, within his Jurisdiction; and his Ships of War, or any Convoys sailing under his Authority, shall upon all occasions, take under their Protection all Vessells belonging to the Subjects, People or Inhabitants of the said United States, or any of them, and holding the same Course, or going the same Way, and shall defend such Vessells as long as they hold the same Course, or go the same Way, against all Attacks, Force, and Violence, in the same manner, as they ought to protect and defend Vessells belonging to the Subjects of the most Christian King.

Art. V. In like manner the said United States, and their Ships of War and Convoys sailing under their Authority shall protect and defend all Vessells and Effects belonging to the Subjects of the most Christian King, and endeavour to recover and restore them, if taken within the Jurisdiction of the said United States, or any of them.

Art. VI. The most Christian King and the said United States shall not receive, nor suffer to be received into any of their Ports, Havens, Roads, Countries, Islands, Cities or Towns, any Pirates, or Sea Robbers, or afford, or suffer any Entertainment, Assistance, or Provisions to be afforded to them, but shall endeavour by all Means, that all Pirates, and Sea Robbers, and their Partners, Sharers, and Abettors be found out, apprehended, and suffer condign Punishment; and all the Vessels and Effects piratically taken, and brought into the Ports or Havens of the most Christian King, or the said United States, which can be found, altho they be Sold, shall be restored, or Satisfaction given therefor to the right owners, their Agents or Attornies demanding the same, and making the right of Property to appear by due Proof.

Art. VII. The most Christian King shall protect, defend and secure, as far as in his Power, the Subjects, People and Inhabitants of the said United States and every of them, and their Vessells and Effects of every Kind, against all Attacks, Assaults, Violences, Injuries, Depredations or Plunderings by or from the King or Emperor of Morocco, or Fez, and the States of Algiers, Tunis and Tripoli, and any of them, and every other Prince, State and Power, on the Coast of Barbary in Africa and the Subjects of the said King, Emperor, States, and Powers, and of every of them, in the same manner, and as effectually and fully, and as much to the Benefit Advantage Ease and Safety of the said united States and every of them, and of the Subjects, People, and Inhabitants thereof, to all Intents and Purposes, as the King and Kingdom of Great Britain, before the Commencement of the present War, protected, defended, and secured the People and Inhabitants of the said United States, then called the British Colonies, in America, their Vessells and Effects, against all such attacks, Assaults, Violences, Injuries, Depredations and Plunderings.

Art. VIII. If, in Consequence of this Treaty, the King of Great Britain, should declare War, against the most Christian King, the said United States shall not assist Great Britain, in such War, with Men, Money, Ships, or any of the Articles in this treaty denominated Contraband Goods.

Art. IX. The most Christian King, shall never invade, nor under any pretence attempt to possess himself of Labradore, New Britain, Nova Scotia, Acadia, Canada, Florida, nor any of the Countries, Cities, or Towns, on the Continent of North America, nor of the Islands of Newfoundland, Cape Breton, St. John's, Anticosti, nor of any other Island lying near to the said Continent, in the Seas, or in any Gulph, Bay, or River, it being the true Intent and meaning of this Treaty, that the said United States, shall have the sole, exclusive, undivided and perpetual Possession of the Countries, Cities, and Towns, on the said Continent, and of all Islands near to it, which now are, or lately were under the Jurisdiction of or Subject to the King or Crown of Great Britain, whenever they shall be united or confederated with the said United States.

Art. X. The subjects, inhabitants, merchants, commanders of ships, masters and mariners, of the states, provinces and dominions of each party, respectively, shall abstain and forbear to fish in all places, possessed, or which shall be possessed by the other party. The most christian king's subjects shall not fish in the havens, bays, creeks, roads, coasts

or places which the said United States hold, or shall hereafter hold; and in like manner, the subjects, people and inhabitants of the said United States shall not fish in the havens, bays, creeks, roads, coasts or places which the most christian king possesses, or shall hereafter possess. And if any ship or vessel shall be found fishing, contrary to the tenor of this treaty, the said ship or vessel, with its lading, proof being made thereof, shall be confiscated.

Art. XI. If in any War, the most Christian King, shall conquer, or get Possession of the Islands in the West Indies, now under the Jurisdiction of the King or Crown of Great Britain, or any of them, or any Dominions of the said King or Crown in any other Parts of the World, the Subjects, People and Inhabitants of the said United States, and every of them, shall enjoy the same Rights, Liberties, Priviledges, Immunities and Exemptions in Trade, Commerce and Navigation, to and from the said Islands, and Dominions, that are mentioned in the Second Article of this Treaty.

Art. XII. It is the true Intent and Meaning of this Treaty, that no higher or other Duties shall be imposed on the Exportation of any Thing of the Growth, Production, or Manufacture of the Islands in the West Indies now belonging or which may hereafter belong to the most Christian King, to the said United States, or any of them, than the lowest that are or shall be imposed on the Exportation thereof to France or to any other Part of the World.

Art. XIII. It is agreed, by and between the said Parties that no Duties whatever shall ever here after be imposed on the Exportation of Molasses, from any of the Islands and Dominions of the most Christian King in the West Indies to any of these United States.

Art. XIV. The Subjects, People, and Inhabitants of the United States, or any of them, being Merchants and residing in France, and their Property, and Effects of every Kind, shall be exempt from the Droit d' Aubaine.

Art. XV. The Merchant Ship of either of the Parties, which shall be making into a Port belonging to the Enemy of the other Ally, and concerning whose Voyage, and the Species of Goods on board her, there shall be just Grounds of Suspicion, shall be obliged to exhibit, as well upon the high Seas as in the Ports and Havens, not only her Passports, but like wise Certificates, expressly shewing that her Goods are not of the Number of those which have been prohibited, as Contraband.

Art. XVI. If by the exhibiting of the above Certificates, the other Party discover there are any of those Sorts of Goods, which are pro-

hibited and declared Contraband, and consigned for a Port under the obedience of his Enemies, it shall not be lawfull to break up the Hatches of such Ship, or to open any Chest, Coffers, Packs, Casks, or any other Vessells found therein or to remove the smallest Parcells of her Goods, whether such Ship belong to the Subjects of France, or the Inhabitants of the said United States, unless the lading be brought on Shore in the Presence of the officers of the Court of Admiralty, and an Inventory thereof made; but there shall be no allowance to sell, exchange, or alienate the same in any manner, untill after that due and lawfull Process shall have been had against such prohibited Goods, and the Courts of Admiralty shall, by a Sentence pronounced, have confiscated the same, saving always as well the Ship itself, as any other Goods found therein, which by this Treaty, are to be esteemed free; neither may they be detained on Pretence of their being as it were infected by the prohibited Goods, much less shall they be confiscated as lawfull Prize: But if not the whole Cargo, but only Part thereof shall consist of prohibited or contraband Goods, and the Commander of the Ship shall be ready and willing to deliver them to the Captor who has discovered them, in such Case the Captor having received those Goods, shall forthwith discharge the Ship, and not hinder her by any Means freely to prosecute the Voyage on which she was bound.

Art. XVII. On the Contrary, it is agreed, that whatever shall be found to be laden by the Subjects and Inhabitants of either Party, on any Ship belonging to the Enemy of the other, or to his Subjects, although it be not of the Sort of prohibited Goods, may be confiscated in the same Manner as if it belonged to the Enemy himself, except such Goods and Merchandise as were put on board such Ship before the Declaration of War, or even after such Declaration, if so be it were done without the Knowledge of such Declaration. So that the Goods of the Subjects or People of either Party, whether they be of the Nature of such as are prohibited, or otherwise which, as is aforesaid, were put on board any Ship belonging to an Enemy before the War, or after the Declaration of it, without the Knowledge of it, shall no wise be liable to Confiscation, but shall well and truly be restored without delay to the Proprietors demanding the same; but so as that if the said Merchandises be contraband, it shall not be any Ways lawfull to carry them afterwards to any Ports belonging to the Enemy.

Art. XVIII. And that more effectual Care may be taken, for the Security of the Subjects, and Inhabitants of both Parties, that they suffer no Injury by the Men of War or Privateers of the other Party, all

the Commanders of the Ships of the most Christian King, and of the said United States and all their Subjects and Inhabitants, shall be forbid, doing any Injury, or Damage to the other Side; and if they act to the contrary, they shall be punished, and shall moreover be bound to make Satisfaction for all matter of Damage, and the Interest thereof, by Reparation, under the Penalty and Obligation of their Person and Goods.

Art. XIX. All Ships, and Merchandises, of what Nature soever, which shall be rescued out of the Hands of any Pirates, or Robbers on the high Seas, shall be brought into some Port of either State, and shall be delivered to the Custody of the officers of that Port, in order to be restored entire to the true Proprietor, as soon as due and sufficient Proof shall be made, concerning the Property, thereof.

Art. XX. It shall be lawful for the Ships of War of either Party, and Privateers, freely to carry whithersoever they please, the Ships and Goods, taken from their Enemies, without being obliged to pay any Duty to the Officers of the Admiralty or any other Judges; nor shall such Prizes be arrested, or seized, when they come to, and enter the Ports of either Party; nor shall the Searchers, or other Officers of those Places search the same, or make Examination concerning the Lawfullness of such Prizes, but they may hoist Sail, at any Time and depart and carry their Prizes to the Place expressed in their Commissions, which the Commanders of such Ships of War shall be obliged to shew. On the Contrary, no Shelter, or Refuge shall be given in their Ports to such as shall have made Prize of the Subjects, People, or Property, of either of the Parties; but if such should come in, being forced by Stress of Weather, or the Danger of the Sea, all proper Means shall be vigorously used, that they go out, and retire from thence as soon as possible.

Art. XXI. If any Ships belonging to either of the Parties, their Subjects or People, shall, within the Coasts, or Dominions of the other, stick upon the sands or be wrecked, or suffer any other Damage, all friendly assistance and Relief shall be given to the Persons Shipwrecked, or such as shall be in danger thereof; and Letters of Safe Conduct shall likewise be given to them for their free and quiet Passage from thence, and the Return of every one to his own Country.

Art. XXII. In Case the Subjects and People of either Party, with their Shipping, whether public, and of War, or private and of Merchants, be forced through Stress of Weather, Pursuit of Pirates or Enemies, or any other urgent Necessity, for Seeking of Shelter and Harbour, to retreat, and enter into any of the Rivers, Creeks, Bays, Havens, Roads, Ports, or Shores, belonging to the other Party; they shall be received

and treated with all Humanity, and Kindness, and enjoy all friendly Protection and Help; and they shall be permitted to refresh and provide themselves, at reasonable Rates, with Victuals and all Things needfull for the Sustenance of their Persons, or Reparation of their Ships, and Conveniency of their Voyage; and they shall no Ways be detained or hindered from returning out of the said Ports or Roads, but may remove and depart when and whither they please, without any Lett or Hindrance;

Art. XXIII. For the better promoting of Commerce on both Sides, it is agreed, that if a War shall break out between the Said two Nations, Six Months, after the Proclamation of War, shall be allowed to the Merchants, in the Cities and Towns where they live, for settling and transporting their Goods and Merchandizes; and if any Thing be taken from them, or any Injury be done them within that Time by either Party, or the People or Subjects of either, full Satisfaction shall be made for the Same.

Art. XXIV. No Subjects of the most Christian King, shall apply for, or take any Commission or Letters of Marque for arming any Ship or Ships to act as Privateers, against the said United States or any of them, or against the Subjects, People, or Inhabitants of the said United States or any of them, or against the Property of any of the Inhabitants of any of them, from any Prince, or State with which the said United States shall be at War. Nor shall any Citizen, Subject, or Inhabitant, of the said United States or any of them, apply for, or take any Commission or Letters of Marque for arming any Ship or Ships to act as Privateers, against the Subjects of the most Christian King or any of them, or the Property of any of them, from any Prince or State, with which the said King shall be at War: And if any Person of either Nation shall take such Commissions or Letters of Marque, he shall be punished as a Pirate.

Art. XXV. It shall not be lawfull for any foreign Privateers not belonging [to the] Subjects of the most Christian King, nor Citizens of the said United States, who have Commissions from any other Prince or State, in Enmity with either Nation, to fit their Ships in the Ports of either the one or the other of the aforesaid Parties, to Sell what they have taken, or in any other manner whatsoever to exchange either Ships, Merchandizes, or any other Lading: neither shall they be allowed even to purchase Victuals, except such as shall be necessary for their going to the next Port of that Prince or State from which they have Commissions.

Art. XXVI. It shall be lawfull for all and Singular the Subjects of the most Christian King, and the Citizens, People, and Inhabitants of the said States, to Sail with their Ships, with all manner of Liberty and Security; no distinction being made, who are the Proprietors of the Merchandizes laden thereon from any Port, to the Places of those who now are, or hereafter shall be at Enmity with the most Christian King, or the United States. It shall likewise be lawfull for the Subjects and Inhabitants aforesaid, to sail with the Ships and Merchandizes aforementioned; and to trade with the same Liberty, and Security from the Places, Ports, and Havens of those who are Enemies of both, or either Party, without any opposition or Disturbance whatsoever, not only directly from the Places of the Enemy aforementioned to neutral Places; but also from one Place belonging to an Enemy, to another Place belonging to an Enemy, whether they be under the Jurisdiction of the same Prince or under Several: And it is hereby Stipulated that free Ships shall also give a Freedom to Goods, and that every Thing shall be deemed to be free and exempt, which shall be found on board the Ships, belonging to the Subjects of either of the Confederates; although the whole Lading or any Part thereof, should appertain to the Enemies of Either, Contraband Goods being always excepted. It is also agreed in like manner, that the same Liberty, be extended to Persons, who are on board a free Ship with this Effect, that although they be Enemies to both or either Party, they are not to be taken out of that free Ship, unless they are Soldiers, and in actual Service of the Enemies.

Art. XXVII. This Liberty of Navigation and Commerce shall extend to all Kinds of Merchandizes, excepting those only which are distinguished by the Name of Contraband: and under this Name of Contraband, or prohibited Goods, shall be comprehended Arms, Great Guns, Bombs with their Fuzees, and other Things belonging to them; Fire Balls, Gunpowder, Match, Cannon Ball, Pikes, Swords, Lances Spears, Halberds, Mortars, Petards, Granadoes, Saltpetre, Musketts, Muskett Balls, Helmets, Head Pieces, Breast Plates, Coats of Mail, and the like Kind of Arms proper for arming Soldiers, Muskett rests, Belts, Horses with their Furniture, and all other war like Instruments whatsoever. These Merchandizes which follow, shall not be reckoned among Contraband or prohibited Goods; that is to Say, all Sorts of Cloths, and all other Manufactures woven of any Wool, Flax, Silk, Cotton, or any other Material whatever; all Kinds of Wearing apparell, together with the Species whereof they are used to be made; Gold and Silver, as well coined as uncoined, Tin, Iron, Lead, Copper, Brass, Coals; as also

Wheat and Barley, and any other Kind of Corn and Pulse; Tobacco, and likewise all manner of Spices; Salted and Smoked Flesh, Salted Fish, Cheese and Butter, Beer, Oils, Wines, Sugars, and all Sorts of Salt; and in general, all Provisions which Serve for the Nourishment of Mankind, and the Sustenance of Life: Furthermore, all kinds of Cotton, Hemp, Flax, Tar, Pitch, Ropes, Cables, Sails, Sail Cloth, Anchors, and any Parts of Anchors; also Ships' Masts, Planks, Boards, and Beams, of what Tree Soever; and all other Things proper either for building or repairing Ships, and all other Goods whatsoever which have not been worked into the Form of any Instrument or Thing prepared for War, by Land or by Sea, shall not be reputed Contraband, much less such as have been already wrought and made up for any other use; all which shall wholly be reckoned among free Goods; as likewise all other Merchandizes and Things which are not comprehended, and particularly mentioned in the foregoing Enumeration of Contraband Goods; So that they may be transported and carried in the freest Manner by the Subjects of both Confederates, even to Places belonging to an Enemy, such Towns and Places being only excepted as are at that time besieged, blocked up, or invested.

Art. XXVIII. To the End that all manner of Dissentions and Quarrells may be avoided and prevented on one Side and the other, it is agreed, that in Case either of the Parties hereto, should be engaged in a War, the Ships and Vessells belonging to the Subjects or People of the other Ally, must be furnished with Sea Letters or Passports, expressing the Name, Property and Bulk of the Ship, as also the Name and Place of Habitation of the Master or Commander of the said Ship, that it may appear thereby, that the Ship really and truly belongs to the Subjects of one of the Parties; which Passports shall be made out and granted according to the Form annexed to this Treaty. They shall likewise be recalled every Year; that is, if the Ship happens to return home within the Space of a Year. It is likewise agreed, that such Ships being laden, are to be provided, not only with Passports as abovementioned, but also with Certificates, containing the Several Particulars of the Cargo, the Place whence the Ship sailed, and whither She is bound; that so it may be known whether any forbidden or contraband Goods, be on board the same; which Certificates shall be made out by the Officers of the Place whence the Ship Set Sail, in the accustomed Form. And if any one shall think it fit or advisable to express in the said Certificates the Persons to whom the Goods on board belong, he may freely do so.

Art. XXIX. The Ships of the Subjects and Inhabitants of either of the Parties, coming upon any Coast belonging to either of the said

Allies, but not willing to enter into Port, or being entered into Port, and not willing to unload their Cargoes, or break Bulk, shall not be obliged to give an Account of their Lading, unless they should be Suspected, upon some manifest Tokens, of carrying to the Enemy of the other Ally, any prohibited Goods called Contraband; And in Case of such manifest Suspicion, the Parties shall be obliged to exhibit in the Ports, their Passports and Certificates, in the manner before Specified.

ART. XXX. If the Ships of the said Subjects, People or Inhabitants of either of the Parties, shall be met with, either Sailing along the Coast, or on the high Seas, by any Ship of War of the other, or by any Privateers, the said Ship of War or Privateers, for the avoiding of any disorder, shall remain out of Cannon Shot, and may send their Boats, on board the Merchant Ship, which they shall so meet with, and may enter her to the Number of two or three Men only, to whom the Master or Commander of such Ship or Vessell shall exhibit his Passport, concerning the Property of the Ship, made out according to the Form inserted in this present Treaty; and the Ship when she shall have shewed such Passport, shall be free and at Liberty to pursue her Voyage, so as it shall not be lawfull to molest or search her in any Manner, or to give her Chace, or force her to quit her intended Course. It is also agreed that all Goods when once put on board the Ship or Vessels of either Parties shall be subject to no farther Visitation, but all Visitation or Search shall be made before Hand; and all prohibited Goods shall be stopt on the Spot, before the same be put on board the Ships or Vessels of the respective State: Nor shall either the Person or Goods of the Subjects of His most christian Majesty or the United States be put under any Arrest or molested by any other Kind of Embargo for that Cause; and only the Subject of that State by whom the said Goods have or shall be prohibited, and shall presume to sell or alienate such sort of Goods, shall be duly punished for the Offence.

The Form of the Sea Letters and Passports, to be given, to Ships and Vessels, according to the twenty-eighth Article

To all who shall See these Presents Greeting: It is hereby made known, that Leave and Permission has been given to Master and Commander of the Ship called of the Town of Burthen Tons or thereabouts, lying at present in the Port and Haven of and bound for and laden with after that his Ship has been visited, and before Sailing, he shall make Oath before the officers who have the Jurisdiction of maritime Affairs, that the said Ship belongs to one or more of the Subjects of

the Act whereof shall be put at the End of these Presents; as likewise that he will keep and cause to be kept by his Crew, on board, the Marine ordinances and Regulations, and enter in the proper Office a List signed and witnessed of the Crew of his Ship, and of all who shall embark, on board her, whom he shall not take on board without the Knowledge and Permission of the officers of the Marine; and in every Port and Haven where he shall enter with his Ship, he shall shew this present Leave to the officers and Judges of the Marine, and shall give a faithfull account to them of what passed and was done during his Voyage, and he shall carry the Colours, Arms, and Ensigns of during his Voyage.

In Witness whereof, We have Signed these Presents, and put the Seal of our Arms thereunto, and caused the Same to be countersigned by at the Day of A. D. .

The Form of the Act containing the Oath

We of the Admiralty of do certify that Master of the Ship named in the above Passport, hath taken the oath mentioned therein.

Done at the Day of A. D. .

The Form of the Certificate to be required of and to be given by the Magistrates or officers of the Customs of the Town and Port in their respective Towns and Ports, to the Ships and Vessells, which Sail from thence, according to the Directions of the 28th Article of this present Treaty

We, Magistrates (or officers of the Customs) of the Town and Port of do certify and attest, that on the Day of the Month of in the Year of our Lord personally appeared before Us, of and declared by a Solemn Oath, that the Ship or Vessell called of about Tons whereof of his usual Place of Habitation, is Master or Commander, does rightfully and properly belong to him and others Subjects of and to them alone: That She is now bound from the Port of to the Port of laden with the Goods and Merchandizes hereunder particularly described and enumerated, that is to Say,

In Witness whereof we have Signed this Certificate, and Sealed it with the Seal of our office. Given the day of the Month of in the Year of our Lord .

INSTRUCTIONS TO THE AGENT.

TUESDAY: SEPTEMBER 24, 1776.

Congress resumed the consideration of the instructions to the agent, and the same being debated by paragraphs, and amended, were agreed to.

INSTRUCTIONS TO

There is delivered to you herewith a Plan of a Treaty with his most Christian Majesty of France,[1] approved of in Congress, on the Part of the United States of America.

It is the wish of Congress that the Treaty should be concluded; and you are hereby instructed to use every Means in your Power for concluding it, ~~exactly~~ conformable to the Plan you have received.

If you shall find that to be impracticable, you are hereby authorised to relax the Demands of the United States, and to enlarge their Offers agreeably to the following Directions:

If his most Christian Majesty[2] shall not consent that the subjects [inhabitants] of the United States shall have the Privileges proposed in the second Article, then the United States ought not to give the Subjects of his most Christian Majesty the Privileges proposed in the first Article; but that the United States shall give to his most Christian Majesty the same Privileges, Liberties, and Immunities at least, and the like Favour in all Things which any foreign Nation the most favoured shall have; provided, his most Christian Majesty shall give to the United States the same Benefits, Privileges and Immunities which any the most

[1] Inserted in the writing of John Hancock. W. C. F.

[2] In the draft the letters A and B are used instead of names. W. C. F.

favoured foreign Nation now has, uses, or enjoys. And, in Case neither of these Propositions of equal Advantages are [is] agreed to, then the whole of the said Articles are to be rejected, ~~without absolutely barring~~ rather than obstruct the further Progress of the Treaty.

The third [fourth] Article must be insisted upon.

The sixth [seventh] Article ought to be obtained, if possible; but should be waived, rather than that the Treaty should be interrupted by insisting upon it: His most Christian Majesty agreeing, nevertheless, to use his Interest and Influence to procure Passes from the States mentioned in this Article for the Vessels of the United States upon the Mediterranean.

The seventh [eighth] Article will probably be attended with some Difficulty. If you find his most Christian Majesty determined not to agree to it, you are empowed to add to it, ~~any of the following Proposals Offers or two of them, or all of them, if one or two of them should be discovered to be unsatisfactory~~

postpon'd

1. I~~f A should undertake an Expedition to recover what she lost in the West Indies during the last War with G. Britain the United States will, in that Expedition, supply France with Provisions if required, and will not supply G. Britain with any.~~

2. ~~The United States will agree to an exclusive Contract in Favour of A. during the Term of   Years, for Masts and Naval Stores, as far as they can spare them.~~

postpon'd

3. ~~The United States will not, upon a Peace with Great Britain, grant to her Terms of Commerce more advantageous than those they will grant to A~~,

agreed

as follows: [That the United States will never be subject, or acknowledge allegiance, or obedience, to the king, crown,

or parliament of Great Britain; nor grant to that nation any exclusive trade; or any advantages, or privileges in trade, more than to his most christian majesty; neither shall any treaty for terminating the present war between the king of Great Britain and the United States, or any war which may be declared by the king of Great Britain against his most christian majesty, in consequence of this treaty, take effect, until the expiration of ~~eight~~ six calendar months after the negotiation for that purpose shall have been duly notified, in the former instance by the United States to his most christian majesty, and in the other instance, by his most christian majesty to the United States; to the end that both these parties may be included in the peace, if they think proper.] [1]

The eleventh and twelfth [twelfth and thirteenth] Articles are to be waived, if you find that the Treaty will be interrupted by insisting on it [them].

You will press the thirteenth [fourteenth] Article; but let not the Fate of the Treaty depend upon obtaining it.

If his most Christian Majesty should be unwilling to agree to the fifteenth [sixteenth] and twenty sixth Articles, you are directed to consent that the Goods and Effects of Enemies, on Board the Ships and Vessels of either Party, shall be liable to Seizure and Confiscation.

The twenty fifth Article is not to be insisted upon.

~~As the Scarcity of Arms, Artillery, and other military Stores is so considerable in the United States~~. You will solicit the Court of France for on immediate Supply of twenty or thirty thousand Muskets and Bayonets, and a large Supply of Ammunition and brass Field Pieces, to be sent under Convoy by France. The United States ~~will~~ engage for the Payment of the Arms, Artillery and Am-

[1] The sentences enclosed in brackets were an amendment in the writing of George Wythe. W. C. F.

munition, and to indemnify France for the Expense of the Convoy.

Engage a few good Engineers in the Service of the United States.

It is highly probably that France means not to let the United States sink in the present Contest. But as the Difficulty of obtaining true Accounts of our Condition may cause an Opinion to be entertained that we are able to support the War on our own Strength and Resources longer than, in fact, we can do, it will be proper for you to press for the immediate and explicit declaration of France in our Favour, upon a Suggestion that a Re-union with Great Britain may be the Consequence of a delay.

Should Spain be disinclined to our Cause, from an Apprehension of Danger to his Dominions in South America, you are empowered to give the strongest Assurances, that that Crown will receive no Molestation from the United States, in the Possession of those Territories.

You will transmit to us the most speedy and full Intelligence of your Progress in this Business, and of any other European Transactions that it may import us to know.

[You are desired to get the best and earliest information that you possibly can of any negotiations that the Court of London may be carrying on for obtaining foreign mercenaries to be sent against these States the next Campaign; and if any such design is in agitation, you will endeavor to prevail with the Court of France to exert its influence in the most effectual manner to prevent the execution of such designs.

~~[If the Court of France cannot be prevailed on to engage in the War with Great Britain for any considerations already proposed in this Treaty, you are hereby authorized to agree as a further inducement, that these United States will wage the war in union with France not make peace with~~

~~Great Britain until the latter France shall gain the possession of those Islands in the West Indies formerly called Nieutral, and which by the Treaty of Paris were ceded to G. Britain: provided France shall make the conquest of these Islands an early object of the War and prosecute the same with sufficient force.~~

[You are desired to obtain, as early as possible, a publick acknowledgment of the Independency of these States on the Crown and Parliament of Great Britain, by the Court of France.] [1]

In conducting this important Business, the Congress have the greatest Confidence in your Address, Abilities, Vigilance, and Attachment to the Interests of the United States; and wish you every Success.[2]

Resolved, That the committee of Secret Correspondence be directed to lay before Congress to Morrow morning, the intelligence they have lately received from abroad.

Resolved, That Thursday next be assigned for appointing an agent, or agents, to transact ~~foreign~~ the business of the United States at the Court of France.

The several matters to this day referred, being postponed,

Adjourned to 10 o'Clock to Morrow.

[1] The paragraphs in brackets were amendments by Richard Henry Lee. W. C. F.

[2] The original, in the writing of James Wilson, with the amendments as just noted, is in the *Papers of the Continental Congress,* No. 47, folio 157. It bears an endorsement: "Report of the Com^{ee} on Instructions, bro't in Septr 10, 1776." W. C. F.

II

THE TREATIES

TREATY OF AMITY AND COMMERCE

TREATY OF ALLIANCE

ACT SEPARATE AND SECRET

Editor's note. The text given here is the reproduction of the original manuscripts in the Department of State. It differs in spelling, accents, capitalisation, punctuation and typographical arrangement from the texts printed in different collections of treaties and particularly from the text in the *Journals of Congress,* vol. XI, p. 419. The following discrepancies are especially worthy of notice. Article 15 of the treaty of amity and commerce reads in the manuscript: de briser les écoutilles des dits navires, *ni* d'ouvrir; ni has disappeared in the printed text. Article 21 reads in the manuscript *la* reparation, aucun obstacle *ni* empêchement; the printed text gives *leur* reparation and aucun obstacle ou empêchement. Article 25 reads: Il sera permis à tous et *un* chacun, the printed text is et *à* chacun. Article 27 reads: toutes *discussions* et querelles, changed to *dissensions* et querelles, probably in order to conform to the English translation *dissentions.* In the form of passports, the word *sujets* was crossed out and the words *citoyens des Etats unis d'Amérique* substituted in another hand in the interline; similarly the words citizens of the U. S. of A. were written in the English text. Finally, in the manuscripts, the plenipotentiaries did not sign under each column, but in an horizontal line, in the following order: Gérard, Franklin, Deane, Lee. Minor corrections to the text of the treaties were evidently made by a printer or proof reader when the texts were printed in the so-called "official" issues. It was thought desirable to give here the text as originally signed and as preserved in the archives of the Department of State.

THE TREATIES.

TREATY OF AMITY AND COMMERCE.

Lewis, by the grace of God king of France and Navarre, to all who shall see these presents, Greeting.

The Congress of the thirteen United States of North America having made known to us, by their plenipotentiaries residing at Paris, their desire to establish between us and our dominions a good understanding, and a perfect correspondence; and having for that purpose proposed to conclude with us a treaty of amity and commerce; and we having thought it our duty to give to the said states a sensible proof of our affection, by a determination to accept of their proposals: For these causes, and other good considerations us thereunto moving, we, reposing, entire confidence in the abilities, experience, zeal, and fidelity for our service of our dear and beloved Conrad Alexander Gérard, royal syndic of the city of Strasburg, and secretary of our council of state, having nominated, appointed and commissioned, and by these presents signed with our hand, do nominate, appoint, and commission him our plenipotentiary, giving him power and special command for us, and in our name, to agree

Louis, par la grace de Dieu, Roy de France et de Navarre, à tous ceux, qui ces présentes lettres verront, Salut.

Le Congrès des treize Etats-Unis de l'Amérique Septentrionale, nous ayant fait connoître par ses Plénipotentiaires résidant à Paris, son désir d'établir avec nous et nos Etats une bonne intelligence, et une parfaite correspondance, et nous ayant à cet effet proposé de conclure avec nous un Traité d'amitié et de commerce, nous avons jugé devoir donner aux dits États-unis, une preuve sensible de notre affection, en nous déterminant à accepter leur Propositions. A ces causes, et autres bonnes considérations à ce nous mouvant, nous confiant entièrement en la capacité et expérience, zèle et fidélité pour notre service de notre cher et ame Conrad Alexandre Gérard, Sindic Royal de la ville de Strasbourg, Secrétaire de notre Conseil d'Etat, nous l'avons nommé commis et Député, et par ces présentes signées de notre main le nommons, commettons et députons notre Plénipotentiaire, lui donnant pouvoir et mandement spécial, pour, en notre nom, arrêter, conclure, et signer, avec les Plénipotentiaires

upon, conclude and sign with the plenipotentiaries of the United States, equally furnished in due form with full power, such treaty, convention, and articles of commerce and navigation, as he shall think proper, willing that he act with the same authority as we might or could act, if we were personally present, and even as though he had more special command than what is herein contained; promising in good faith and on the word of a king, to agree to, confirm, and establish forever, and to accomplish and execute punctually, all that our said dear and beloved Conrad Alexander Gérard shall stipulate and sign, by virtue of the present power, without contravening it in any manner, or suffering it to be contravened for any cause, or under any pretext whatsoever; and also to ratify the same in due form, and cause our ratification to be delivered and exchanged in the time that shall be agreed on. For such is our pleasure.

In testimony whereof, we have hereunto set our seal.

Done at Versailles, this thirtieth day of January, in the year of our Lord, one thousand seven hundred and seventy-eight, and the fourth year of our reign.

[L. S.] Signed, LOUIS.

By the King.

GRAVIER DE VERGENNES.

des États-unis, munis également de leurs pouvoirs en bonne forme, tels Traité, Convention, et Articles de Commerce et de Navigation qu'il avisera bon être; voulant qu'il agisse avec la même autorité, que nous ferions ou pourrions faire si nous étions présents en personne, encore qu'il y eût quelque chose qui requit un mandement plus spécial, que ce qui est contenu en ces présentes. Promettant en foi et parole de Roi d'avoir agréable, tenir ferme et stable à toujours, accomplir et exécuter ponctuellement tout ce que notre dit cher et amé Conrad Alexandre Gérard aura stipulé et signé en vertu du present Pouvoir, sans jamais y contrevenir, ni permettre qu'il y soit contrevenu, pour quelque cause et sous quelque prétexte que ce puisse être; comme aussi d'en faire expédier nos Lettres de Ratification en bonne forme, et de les faire delivrer, pour être échangées dans le temps dont il sera convenu. CAR TEL EST NOTRE PLAISIR. En témoin de quoi nous avons fait mettre notre Scel à ces présentes. Donné à Versailles, ce trentième jour du mois de Janvier, l'an de grâce, mil sept cent soixante et dix huit, et de notre règne, le quatrième.

[L. S.] LOUIS.

Par le Roy

GRAVIER DE VERGENNES.[1]

[1] A copy of these powers, in the writing of Benjamin Franklin, is in the Departmen of State. W. C. F.

TREATY
OF AMITY AND COMMERCE.

The most Christian King, and the thirteen United States of North America, to wit, New-Hampshire, Massachusetts Bay, Rhodeisland, Connecticut, New York, New-Jersey, Pennsylvania, Delaware, Maryland, Virginia, North-Carolina, South Carolina, & Georgia, willing to fix in an equitable and permanent manner the Rules which ought to be followed relative to the Correspondence & Commerce which the two Parties desire to establish between their respective Countries, States, and Subjects, his most Christian Majesty and the said United States have judged that the said End could not be better obtained than by taking for the Basis of their Agreement the most perfect Equality and Reciprocity, and by carefully avoiding all those burthensome Preferences, which are usually Sources of Debate, Embarrasment and Discontent; by leaving also each Party at Liberty to make, respecting Commerce and Navigation, those interior Regulations which it shall find most convenient to itself; and by founding the Advantage of Commerce solely upon reciprocal Utility, and the just Rules of free Intercourse; reserving withal to each Party the Liberty of admitting at its pleasure other Nations to a Participation of the same Advantages. It is in the Spirit of this Intention, and to fulfil these Views, that

TRAITÉ
D'AMITIÉ ET DE COMMERCE

Le Roi Très chretien et les treize Etats-unis de l'Amérique septentrionale, savoir, Newhampshire La Baye de Massachusset, Rhode-Island, Connecticut, New York, New Jersey, Pensylvanie, Les Comtés de Newcastle de Kent et de Sussex sur la Delaware, Maryland, Virginie, Caroline septentrionale, Caroline Méridionale et Georgie, voulant établir d'une maniere équitable et permanente les règles qui devront être suivies relativement à la Correspondance et au Commerce que les deux parties désirent d'établir entre leurs Païs, Etats et sujets respectifs, Sa Majesté Très chretienne et le dits Etats unis ont jugé ne pouvoir mieux atteindre à ce but qu'en prenant pour base de leur arrangement l'égalité et la réciprocité la plus parfaite, et en observant d'éviter toutes les préférences onéreuses, source de discussions, d'embarras et de mecontentemens, de laisser à chaque partie la liberté de faire relativement au Commerce et à la Navigation les réglemens intérieurs qui seront à sa convenance, de ne fonder les avantages du Commerce que sur son utilité reciproque et sur les loix d'une juste concurrence, et de conserver ainsi de part et d'autre la liberté de faire participer, chacun selon son gré, les autres Nations aux mêmes avantages. C'est dans cet esprit et pour remplir ces vües que

his said Majesty having named and appointed for his Plenipotentiary Conrad Alexander Gerard, Royal *Sindic* of the City of Strasbourg, Secretary of His Majesty's Council of State, and the United States on their Part, having fully impower'd Benjamin Franklin Deputy from the State of Pennsylvania to the general Congress, and President of the Convention of said State, Silas Deane late Deputy from the State of Connecticut to the said Congress, and Arthur Lee Councellor at Law; The said respective Plenipotentiaries after exchanging their Powers, and after mature Deliberation, have concluded and agreed upon the following Articles.

Article 1st.

There shall be a firm, inviolable and universal Peace, and a true and sincere Friendship between the most Christian King, his Heirs and Successors, and the United States of America; and the Subjects of the most Christian King * and of the said United States, and the People and Inhabitants of every Degree, without exception of Persons or Places; & the Terms herein after mentioned shall be perpetual between the most Christian King his Heirs and Successors and the said United States.

* and of the said States; and between the Countries, Islands, Cities, and Towns, situate under the Jurisdiction of the most Christian King,

Sa d^{e}. Majesté ayant nommé et constitué pour son Plenipotentiaire le S. Conrad Alexandre Gerard, Sindic Roïal de la Ville de Strasbourg, Secretaire du Conseil d'Etat de Sa Majesté, et les Etats unis aïant, de leur coté, munis de leurs pleins pouvoirs les S^{rs}. Benjamin Franklin Député au Congrès général de la part de l'Etat de Pensylvanie et Président de la Convention du d^{e}. Etat, Silas Deane ci-devant Député de l'Etat de Connecticut, et Arthur Lée, *Conseiller ès loix,* Les d^{s}. Plénipotentiaires respectifs après l'échange de leurs pouvoirs et après mure déliberation ont conclu et arrêté les points et articles suivans.

Art. 1er.

Il y aura une paix ferme, inviolable et universelle et une amitié vraie et sincère entre le Roi Très chrétien, ses héritiers et successeurs, et entre les Etats unis de l'Amérique ainsi qu'entre les sujets de Sa Majesté Très chretienne et ceux des dits Etats, comme aussi entre les peuples Isles, Villes et places situés sous la Jurisdiction du Roi Très chretien et des dits Etats unis, et entre leurs peuples et habitans de toutes les classes, sans aucune exception de personnes et de lieux; les conditions mentionnées au present Traité seront perpetuelles et permanentes entre le Roi très Chretien, ses héritiers et successeurs et les dits Etats unis.

ART. 2ND.

The most Christian King, and the United States engage mutually not to grant any particular Favour to other Nations in respect of Commerce and Navigation, which shall not immediately become common to the other Party, who shall enjoy the same Favour, freely, if the Concession was freely made, or on allowing the same Compensation, if the Concession was Conditional.

ART. 2.

Le Roi Très chretien et les Etats unis s'engagent mutuellement à n'accorder aucune faveur particulière à d'autres Nations en fait de Commerce et de Navigation qui ne devienne aussitôt commune à l' autre partie, et celle ci jouira de cette faveur gratuitement, si la concession est gratuite, ou en accordant la même compensation si la concession est conditionnelle.

ART. 3D.

The Subjects of the most Christian King shall pay in the Ports, Havens, Roads, Countries Islands, Cities or Towns, of the United States or any of them, no other or greater Duties or Imposts, of what Nature soever they may be, or by what Name soever called, than those which the Nations most favoured are or shall be obliged to pay; and they shall enjoy all the Rights, Liberties, Privileges, Immunities and Exemptions in Trade, Navigation and Commerce, whether in passing from one Port in the said States to another, or in going to and from the same, from and to any Part of the World, which the said Nations do or shall enjoy.

ART. 3.

Les sujets du Roi Très chretien ne paieront dans les Ports, havres, rades Contrées, Isles, cités et lieux des Etats unis ou d'aucun d'entr'eux d'autres ni plus grands droits ou impôts, de quelque nature qu'ils puissent être, et quelque nom qu'ils puissent avoir, que ceux que les Nations les plus favorisées sont, ou seront tenües de païer; Et ils jouiront de tous les droits, libertés, priviléges immunités et exemtions en fait de négoce, navigation et commerce, soit en passant d'un Port des dits Etats à un autre, soit en y allant ou en revenant de quelque partie ou pour quelque partie du Monde que ce soit, dont les d^{es}. Nations jouissent ou jouiront.

ART. 4.

The Subjects, People and Inhabitants of the said United States, and each of them, shall not pay in the Ports, Havens Roads, Isles,

ART. 4.

Les sujets peuples et habitans des d. Etats-unis et de chacun d'iceux ne païeront dans les Ports, havres, rades, Isles, villes et places de la

Cities & Places under the Domination of his most Christian Majesty in Europe, any other or greater Duties or Imposts, of what Nature soever, they may be, or by what Name soever called, than those which the most favour'd Nations are or shall be obliged to pay; & they shall enjoy all the Rights, Liberties, Privileges, Immunities & Exemptions, in Trade, Navigation and Commerce, whether in passing from one Port in the said Dominions in Europe to another, or in going to and from the same, from and to any Part of the World, which the said Nations do or shall enjoy.

Domination de Sa Majesté Très chretienne en Europe d'autres ni plus grands droits ou impots de quelque nature qu'ils puissent être et quelque nom qu'ils puissent avoir que les Nations les plus favorisées sont ou seront tenües de païer, et ils jouiront de tous les droits, libertés priviléges immunités et exemtions en fait de négoce, navigation et commerce soit en passant d'un port à un autre des d^s^. Etats du Roi Très chretien en Europe, soit en y allant ou en revenant de quelque partie ou pour quelque partie du monde que ce soit dont les Nations susd^es^. jouissent ou jouiront.

Art. 5.

In the above Exemption is particularly comprised the Imposition of 100 Sols Pr Ton, established in France on foreign Ships; unless when the Ships of the United States shall load with the Merchandize of France for another Port of the same Dominion, in which Case the said Ships shall pay the Duty above mentioned so long as other Nations the most favour'd shall be obliged to pay it. But it is understood that the said United States or any of them are at Liberty when they shall judge it proper, to establish a Duty equivalent in the same Case.

Art. 5.

Dans l'exemtion ci dessus est nommément compris l'imposition de cent sous par Tonneau établie en France sur les Navires étrangers, si ce n'est lorsque les Navires des Etats-unis chargeront des marchandises de France dans un port de France pour un autre port de la même Domination auquel cas les d^s^. Navires des d^s^. Etats-unis acquiteront le droit dont il s'agit aussi longtems que les autres Nations les plus favorisées seront obligées de l'acquiter. Bien entendu qu'il sera libre aux dits Etats unis ou à aucun d'iceux d'établir, quand ils le jugeront àpropos, un droit equivalent à celui dont il est question pour le même cas pour lequel il est etabli dans les Ports de Sa Majeste Très chretienne.

ART. 6.

The most Christian King shall endeavour by all the means in his Power to protect and defend all Vessels and the Effects belonging to the Subjects, People or Inhabitants of the said United States, or any of them, being in his Ports, Havens or Roads or on the Seas near to his Countries, Islands, Cities or Towns and to recover and restore to the right owners, their agents or Attornies all such Vessels & Effects, which shall be taken within his Jurisdiction; and the Ships of War of his most Christian Majesty or any Convoys sailing under his authority shall upon all Occasions take under their Protection all Vessels belonging to the Subjects, People or Inhabitants of the said United States, or any of them & holding the same Course or going the same Way, and shall defend such Vessels, as long as they hold the same Course or go the same way, against all Attacks, Force and Violence in the same manner, as they ought to protect and defend the Vessels belonging to the Subjects of the most Christian King.

ART. 6.

Le Roi Très Chretien fera usage de tous les moïens qui sont en son pouvoir pour protéger et défendre tous les Vaisseaux et effets apartenants aux sujets, peuples et habitans des dits Etats-unis et de chacun d'iceux qui seront dans ses ports, havres ou rades ou dans les Mers près de ses Pays, Contrées, Isles, Villes et places, et fera tous ses efforts pour recouvrer et faire restituer aux propriétaires légitimes, leurs Agens ou Mandataires, tous les vaisseaux et effets qui leur seront pris dans l'étendüe de sa jurisdiction; Et les Vaisseaux de guerre de Sa Majesté Très chretienne ou les convois quelconques faisant voile sous son autorité, prendront, en toute occasion, sous leur protection tous les Vaisseaux apartenants aux sujets peuples et habitans des ds Etats unis ou d'aucun d'iceux, les quels tiendront le meme cours et feront la même route, et ils défendront les dits Vaisseaux aussi longtems qu'ils tiendront le même cours et suivront la meme route, contre toute attaque force ou violence de la même manière qu'ils sont tenus de défendre et de protéger les Vaisseaux appartenans aux sujets de Sa Majesté Très chretienne.

ART. 7.

In like manner the said United States and their Ships of War sail-

ART. 7.

Pareillement des dits Etats unis et leurs Vaisseaux de guerre faisant

ing under their Authority shall protect and defend, conformable to the Tenor of the preceeding Article, all the Vessels and Effects * that shall have been taken within the Jurisdiction of the said United States or any of them.

* belonging to the Subjects of the most Christian King; and use all their Endeavours to recover & cause to be restored the said Vessels & Effects.

voile sous leur autorité protégeront et défendront conformement au contenu de l'art^e^. précédent, tous les Vaisseaux et effets apartenants aux sujets du Roi Très Chretien, et feront tous leurs efforts pour recouvrer et faire restitüer les dits Vaisseaux et effets qui auront été pris dans l'étendüe de la Jurisdiction des dits Etats et de chacun d'iceux.

ART. 8.

The most Christian King will employ his good Offices and Interposition with the King or Emperor of Morocco or Fez, the Regencies of Algier, Tunis and Tripoli, or with any of them, and also with every other Prince, State or Power of the Coast of Barbary in Africa, and the Subjects of the said King Emperor, States and Powers, and each of them; in order to provide as fully and efficaciously as possible for the Benefit, Conveniency and Safety of the said United States, and each of them, their Subjects, People, and Inhabitants, and their Vessels and Effects, against all Violence, Insult, Attacks, or Depredations on the Part of the said Princes and States of Barbary, or their Subjects.

ART. 8.

Le Roi Très chretien emploïera ses bons offices et son entremise auprès des Roi ou Empereur de Maroc ou Fez, des Regences d'Alger, Tunis et Tripoli ou auprès aucune d'entr Elles, ainsi qu'auprès de tout autre Prince Etat ou Puissance des côtes de Barbarie en Affrique et des sujets des d^s^. Roi, Empereur, Etats et Puissance et de chacun d'iceux à l'effet de pourvoir aussi pleinement et aussi efficacement qu'il sera possible, à l'avantage, commodité et sûreté des dits Etats-unis et de chacun d'iceux, ainsi que de leurs sujets, peuples et habitans, leurs Vaisseaux et effets contre toute violence, insulte, attaque ou déprédations de la part des d^s^. Princes et Etats Barbaresques ou de leurs sujets.

Art. 9.

The Subjects, Inhabitants, Merchants, Commanders of Ships, Masters and Mariners of the States, Provinces and Dominions of each Party respectively, shall abstain and forbear to fish in all Places possessed or which shall be possessed by the other Party: The most Christian Kings Subjects shall not fish in the Havens, Bays, Creeks, Roads Coasts or Places, which the * most Christian King possesses or shall hereafter possess; and if any Ship or Vessel shall be found fishing contrary to the Tenor of this Treaty, the said Ship or Vessel with its lading, proof being made thereof, shall be confiscated. It is however understood, that the Exclusion stipulated in the present Article shall take place only so long, and so far as the most Christian King or the United States shall not in this respect have granted an Exemption to some other Nation.

* said united States hold or shall hereafter hold; and in like manner the Subjects, People and Inhabitants of the said United States shall not fish in the Havens Bays, Creeks, Roads, Coasts or Places, which the

Art. 9.

Les sujets habitans, marchands, Commandans des Navires, Maitres et gens de Mer des Etats, Provinces et Domaines des deux parties s'abstiendront et éviteront reciproquement, de pêcher dans toutes les places possédées ou qui seront possedées par l'autre partie. Les sujets de Sa Majesté Très Chretienne ne pêcheront pas dans les havres, Bayes, Criques, rades, côtes et places que les dits Etats-unis possédent ou possédederont à l'avenir, et de la même manière les sujets, peuples et habitans des d[s]. Etats unis ne pêcheront pas dans les havres, Bayes, Criques, rades, Côtes et places que Sa Majesté Très chretienne posséde actuellement ou possédera à l'avenir, et si quelque Navire ou Batiment étoit surpris pêchant en violation du present Traité, le dit Navire ou Batiment et sa Cargaison seront confisqués, après que la preuve en aura été faite düement. Bien entendu que l'exclusion stipulée dans le present article n'aura lieu qu'autant et si longtems que le Roi et les Etats unis n'auront point accordé à cet egard d'exception à quelque Nation que ce puisse être.

Art. 10.

The United States their Citizens and Inhabitants shall never disturb the Subjects, of the most

Art. 10.

Les Etats unis, leurs Citoïens et habitans ne troubleront jamais les sujets du Roi Très chretien dans

Christian King in the Enjoyment and Exercise of the Right of Fishing on the Banks of Newfoundland; nor in the indefinite and exclusive Right which belongs to them on that Part of the Coast of that Island which is designed by the Treaty of Utrecht; nor in the Rights relative to all and each of the Isles which belong to his most Christian Majesty; the whole conformable to the true Sense of the Treaties of Utrecht and Paris.

la jouissance et exercice du droit de pêche sur les bancs de Terreneuve, non plus que dans la jouissance indéfinie et exclusive qui leur apartient sur la partie des Côtes de cette Isle designée dans le Traite d'Utrecht ni dans les droits relatifs à toutes et chacune des Isles qui appartiennent à Sa Majesté très Chretienne. Le tout conformement au véritable sens des Traités d'Utrecht et de Paris.

ART. 11.

It is agreed and concluded that there shall never be any Duty imposed on the Exportation of the Mellasses that may be taken by the Subjects of any of the United States from the Islands of America which belong or may hereafter appertain to his most Christian Majesty.

ART. 11.*

Il est convenu et arrêté qu'il ne sera jamais imposé aucun droit sur l'exportation des Melasses qui pourront être tirées par les sujets d'aucun des Etats-unis des Isles d'Amérique qui appartiennent ou pourront apartenir à Sa Majesté très Chretienne.

* to be omitted, & the subsequent numbers changed accordingly. *Marginal note.*

ART. 12.

In compensation of the Exemption stipulated by the preceeding Article, it is agreed and concluded that there shall never be any Duties imposed on the Exportation of any kind of Merchandize which the Subjects of his most Christian Majesty may take from the Countries and Possessions present or future of any of the thirteen United States, for the Use of the Islands which shall furnish Mellasses.

ART. 12.

En compensation de l'exemtion stipulée par l'article précédent, il est convenu et arrêté qu'il ne sera jamais imposé aucun droit sur l'exportation d'aucune espèce de denrées et marchandises que les sujets de Sa Majesté Très Chretienne pourront tirer des Pays ou possessions actuelles ou futures d'aucun des Treize Etats-unis pour l'usage des Isles qui fournissent les melasses.

Art. 13.

The Subjects and Inhabitants of the said United States, or any one of them, shall not be reputed Aubains in France, & consequently shall be exempted from the *Droit d'Aubaine* or other similar Duty under what name soever. They may by Testament, Donation, or otherwise dispose of their Goods moveable and immoveable in favour of such Persons as to them shall seem good; and their Heirs, Subjects of the said United States, residing whether in France or elsewhere, may succeed them *ab intestat,* without being obliged to obtain Letters of Naturalization, and without having the Effect of this Concession contested or impeded under Pretext of any Rights or Prerogatives of Provinces, Cities, or Private Persons. And the said Heirs, whether such by particular Title, or *ab intestat,* shall be exempt from all Duty called *Droit de Detraction,* or other Duty of the same kind; saving nevertheless, the local Rights or Duties as much and as long as similar ones are not established by the United States or any of them. The Subjects of the most Christian King shall enjoy on their Part, in all the Dominions of the sd States, an entire and perfect Reciprocity relative to the Stipulations contained in the present Article.

Art. 13.

Les sujets et habitans des dits Etats-unis ou de l'un d'eux ne seront point reputés Aubains en France et conséquemment seront exemts du droit d'aubaine ou autre droit semblable quelque nom qu'il puisse avoir; pourront disposer par Testament, Donation, ou autrement de leurs biens meubles et immeubles en faveur de telles personnes que bon leur semblera; Et leurs héritiers, sujets des dits Etats-unis, residans soit en France soit ailleurs, pourront leur succéder *ab intestat,* sans qu'ils aïent besoin d'obtenir des lettres de naturalité, et sans que l'effet de cette concession leur puisse être contesté ou empêché sous pretexte de quelques droits ou prérogatives des Provinces, Villes, ou personnes privées. Et seront les dits héritiers, soit à titre particulier, soit *ab intestat* exemts de tout droit de détraction ou autre droit de ce genre, sauf néanmoins les droits locaux, tant et si longtems qu'il n'en sera point etabli de pareils par les dits Etats-unis ou aucun d'iceux. Les sujets du Roi Très chretien jouiront de leur côté, dans tous les Domaines des dits Etats d'une entière et parfaite reciprocité relativement aux stipulations renfermées dans le present article.

But it is at the same Time agreed that its Contents shall not affect the Laws made or that may be made hereafter in France against Emigrations, which shall remain in all their Force and Vigour; and the United States on their Part, or any of them, shall be at Liberty to enact such Laws relative to that Matter, as to them shall seem proper.

Mais il est convenu en même tems que son contenu ne portera aucune atteinte aux loix promulguées en France contre les émigrations, ou qui pourront être promulguées dans la suite, les quelles demeureront dans toute leur force et vigueur. Les Etats-unis de leur côté ou aucun d'entr'eux, seront libres de statüer sur cette matière telle loi qu'ils jugeront àpropos.

ART. 14.

The merchant Ships of either of the Parties, which shall be making into a Port belonging to the Enemy of the other Ally and concerning whose Voyage & the Species of Goods on board her there shall be just Grounds of Suspicion shall be obliged to exhibit as well upon the high Seas as in the Ports and Havens not only her Passports, but likewise Certificates expressly shewing that her Goods are not of the Number of those, which have been prohibited as contraband.

ART. 14.

Les Navires Marchands des deux parties qui seront destinés pour des Ports appartenants à une Puissance ennemie de l'autre allié, et dont le voïage ou la nature des marchandises dont ils seront chargés donneroit de justes soupçons, seront tenus d'exhiber, soit en haute Mer, soit dans les Ports et havres nonseulement leurs passeports, mais encore les Certificats qui constateront expressement que leur chargement n'est pas de la qualité de ceux qui sont prohibés comme contrebande.

ART. 15.

If by the exhibiting of the above-said Certificates, the other Party discover there are any of those Sorts of Goods, which are prohibited and declared contraband and consigned for a Port under the Obedience of his Enemies, it shall not be Lawful to break up the Hatches of such Ship, or to open

ART. 15.

Si l'exhibition des dits Certificats conduit à découvrir que le Navire porte des marchandises prohibées et reputées contrebande consignées pour un Port ennemi, il ne sera pas permis de briser les écoutilles desdits Navires, ni d'ouvrir aucune Caisse, Coffre, Malle, Ballots, Tonneaux, et autres Caisses

any Chest, Coffers, Packs, Casks, or any other Vessels found therein, or to remove the smallest Parcels of her Goods, whether such Ship belongs to the Subjects of France or the Inhabitants of the said United States, unless the lading be brought on Shore in the presence of the Officers of the Court of Admiralty and an Inventory thereof made; but there shall be no allowance to sell, exchange, or alienate the same in any manner, untill after that due and lawful Process shall have been had against such prohibited Goods, and the Court of Admiralty shall, by a Sentence pronounced, have confiscated the same: saving always as well the Ship itself as any other Goods found therein, which by this Treaty are to be esteemed free: * But if not the whole Cargo, but only part thereof shall consist of prohibited or contraband Goods and the Commander of the Ship shall be ready and willing to deliver them to the Captor, who has discovered them, in such Case the Captor having received those Goods shall forthwith discharge the Ship and not hinder her by any means freely to prosecute the Voyage, on which she was bound. But in Case the Contraband Merchandises, cannot be all receiv'd on board the Vessel of the Captor, then the Captor may, notwithstanding the Offer of delivering him the Contraband Goods, carry

qui s'y trouveront, ou d'en déplacer et détourner la moindre partie des marchandises, soit que le Navire apartienne aux sujets du Roi Très Chretien ou aux habitans des Etats unis jusqu'a ce que la Cargaison ait été mise à terre en presence des Officiers des Cours d'Amirauté, et que l'Inventaire en ait ete fait; mais on ne permettra pas de vendre, échanger ou aliéner les Navires ou leur Cargaison en manière quelconque avant que le procès ait été fait et parfait legalement pour déclarer la contrebande, et que les Cours d'Amirauté auront prononcé leur confiscation par Jugement sans préjudice néanmoins des Navires ainsi que des marchandises, qui, en vertu du Traité doivent être censées libres. Il ne sera pas permis de retenir ces marchandises sous pretexte qu' elles ont été entachées par les marchandises de Contrebande, et bien moins encore de les confisquer comme des prises légales. Dans le cas où une partie seulement et non la totalité du chargement consisteroit en marchandises de Contrebande, et que le Commandant du Vaisseau consente à les délivrer au Corsaire qui les aura découverts, àlors le Capitaine qui aura fait la prise après avoir reçu ces marchandises doit incontinent relâcher le Navire et ne doit l'empêcher, en aucune manière, de continuer son voïage. Mais dans le cas où les marchandises de contrebande ne

the Vessel into the nearest Port agreable to what is above directed.

* neither may they be detained on pretence of their being as it were infected by the prohibited Goods, much less shall they be confiscated as lawful Prize:

pourroient pas être toutes chargées sur le Vaisseau Capteur, àlors le Capitaine du d. Vaisseau sera le Maitre, malgré l'offre de remettre la contrebande, de conduire le patron dans le plus prochain port, conformement à ce qui est préscrit plus haut.

Art. 16.

On the contrary it is agreed, that whatever shall be found to be laden by the Subjects and Inhabitants of either Party on any Ship belonging to the Enemys of the other or to their Subjects, the whole although it be not of the Sort of prohibited Goods may be confiscated in the same manner, as if it belonged to the Enemy, except such Goods and Merchandizes as were put on board such Ship before the Declaration of War, or even after such Declaration, if so be it were done without knowledge of such Declaration. So that the Goods of the Subjects and People of either Party, whether they be of the Nature of such as are prohibited or otherwise, which, as is aforesaid were put on board any Ship belonging to an Enemy before the War, or after the Declaration of the same, without the Knowledge of it, shall no ways be liable to confiscation, but shall well and truely be restored without Delay to the proprietors demanding the same; but so as that, if the said Merchandizes be contraband, it shall not

Art. 16.

On est convenu au contraire que tout ce qui se trouvera chargé par les sujets respectifs sur des Navires apartenants aux ennemis de l'autre partie, ou à leurs sujets sera confisqué sans distinction des marchandises prohibées ou non prohibées, ainsi et de même qui si elles apartenoient à l'ennemi, à l'exception toutefois des effets et marchandises qui auront été mis à bord des dits navires avant la déclaration de guerre, ou même après la d[e]. déclaration, si au moment du chargement on a pu l'ignorer, de manière que les marchandises des sujets des deux parties, soit qu'elles se trouvent du nombre de celles de contrebande ou autrement, les quelles comme il vient d'être dit auront été mises à bord, d'un Vaisseau apartenant à l'ennemi avant la guerre ou même après la d[e]. dèclaration, lorsqu'on l'ignoroit ne seront, en aucune manière, sujetes à confiscation, mais seront fidèlement et de bonne foi rendües sans delai à leurs propriétaires qui les reclameront; bien entendu néanmoins

be any Ways lawful to carry them afterwards to any Ports belonging to the Enemy. The two contracting Parties agree, that the Term of two Months being passed after the Declaration of War, their respective Subjects, from whatever Part of the World they come, shall not plead the Ignorance mentioned in this Article.

qu'il ne soit pas permis de porter dans les Ports ennemis les marchandises qui seront de contrebande. Les deux parties contractantes conviennent que le terme de deux mois passés depuis la déclaration de guerre, leurs sujets respectifs, de quelque partie du monde qu'ils viennent ne pourront plus alléguer l'ignorance dont il est question dans le present article.

ART. 17.

And that more effectual Care may be taken for the Securitye of the Subjects and Inhabitants of both Parties, that they suffer no injury by the men of War or Privateers of the other Party, all the Commanders of the Ships of his most Christian Majesty & of the said United States and all their Subjects and Inhabitants shall be forbid doing any Injury or Damage to the other Side; and if they act to the contrary, they shall be punished and shall moreover be bound to make Satisfaction for all Matter of Damage, and the Interest thereof, by reparation, under the Pain and obligation of their Person and Goods.

ART. 17.

Et afin de pourvoir plus efficacement à la sûreté des sujets des deux parties contractantes, pour qu'il ne leur soit fait aucun prejudice par les Vaisseaux de guerre de l'autre partie ou par des Armateurs particuliers, il sera fait défense à tous Capitaines des Vaisseaux de Sa Majesté très Chretienne et des dits Etats-unis, et à tous leurs sujets de faire aucun dommage ou insulte à ceux de l'autre partie, et au cas où ils y contreviendroient, ils en seront punis et de plus ils seront tenus et obligés en leurs personnes et en leurs biens de reparer tous les dommages et intérêts.

ART. 18.

All Ships and Merchandizes of what Nature soever which shall be rescued out of the Hands of any Pirates or Robbers on the high Seas, shall be brought into some Port of

ART. 18.

Tous Vaisseaux et marchandises de quelque nature que ce puisse être, lorsqu'ils auront été enlevés des mains de quelques Pirates en pleine Mer. seront amenés dans

either State and shall be delivered to the Custody of the Officers of that Port, in order to be restored entire to the true Proprietor as soon as due and sufficient Proof shall be made concerning the Property thereof.

ART. 19.

It shall be lawful for the Ships of War of either Party & Privateers freely to carry whithersoever they please the Ships and Goods taken from their Enemies, without being obliged to pay any Duty to the Officers of the Admiralty or any other Judges; nor shall such Prizes be arrested or seized, when they come to and enter the Ports of either Party; nor shall the Searchers or other Officers of those Places search the same or make examination concerning the Lawfulness of such Prizes, but they may hoist Sail at any time and depart and carry their Prizes to the Places express'd in their Commissions, which the Commanders of such Ships of War shall be obliged to shew: On the contrary no Shelter or Refuge shall be given in their Ports to such as shall have made Prize of the Subjects, People or Property of either of the Parties; but if such shall come in, being forced by Stress of Weather or the Danger of the Sea, all proper means shall be vigorously used that they go out and retire from thence as soon as possible.

quelque Port de l'un des deux Etats, et seront remis à la garde des Officiers du d. Port, âfin d'être rendus, en entier, a leur veritable propriétaire, aussitôt qu'il aura düement et sufisament fait conster de sa propriété.

ART. 19.

Les vaisseaux de guerre de Sa Majesté Très Chretienne et ceux des Etats-unis, de même que ceux que leurs sujets auront armés en guerre, pourront, en toute liberté, conduire où bon leur semblera les prises qu'ils auront faites sur leurs ennemis, sans être obligés à aucuns droits, soit des Sieurs Amiraux ou de l'Amirauté, où d'aucuns autres, sans qu'aussi les dits Vaisseaux ou les d^{es}. prises, entrant dans les havres ou Ports de Sa Majesté Très Chretienne ou des dits Etats-unis puissent être arrêtés ou saisis, ni que les Officiers des lieux puissent prendre connoissance de la validité des d^{es}. prises, les quelles pourront sortir et être conduites franchement et en toute liberté aux lieux portés par les Commissions dont les Capitaines des dits Vaisseaux seront obligés de faire aparoir. Et au contraire ne sera donné asile ni retraite dans leurs ports ou havres à ceux qui auront fait des prises sur les sujets de Sa Majesté ou des dits Etats unis; Et s'ils sont forcés d'y entrer par tempête ou peril de la Mer, on les fera sortir le plustôt qu'il sera possible.

Art. 20.

If any Ship belonging to either of the Parties their People or Subjects, shall, within the Coasts or Dominions of the other, stick upon the Sands or be wrecked or suffer any other Damage, all friendly Assistance and Relief shall be given to the Persons shipwrecked or such as shall be in danger thereof; and Letters of safe Conduct shall likewise be given to them for their free and quiet Passage from thence, and the return of every one to his own Country.

Art. 20.

Dans le cas où un vaisseau apartenant à l'un des deux Etats ou à leurs sujets, aura échoué, fait naufrage ou souffert quelqu'autre dommage sur les Côtes ou sous la Domination de l'une des deux parties, il sera donné toute aide et assistance amiable aux personnes naufragées ou qui se trouvent en danger, et il leur sera accordé des sauf conduits pour assûrer leur passage et leur retour dans leur patrie.

Art. 21.

In Case the Subjects and Inhabitants of either Party with their shipping whether publick and of War or private and of Merchants, be forced, through Stress of Weather, pursuit of Pirates or Enemies, or any other urgent necessity for seeking of Shelter and Harbour, to retreat and enter into any of the Rivers, Bays, Roads or Ports belonging to the other Party, they shall be received and treated with all humanity and Kindness and enjoy all friendly Protection & Help; and they shall be permitted to refresh and provide themselves at reasonable Rates with victuals and all things needful for the sustenance of their Persons or reparation of their Ships and conveniency of their Voyage; and they shall no Ways be detained

Art. 21.

Lorsque les sujets et habitans de l'une des deux parties avec leurs vaisseaux soit publics et de guerre, soit particuliers et marchands, seront forcés par une tempête, par la poursuite des Pirates et des ennemis, ou par quelqu'autre nécessité urgente de chercher refuge et un abri, de se retirer et entrer dans quelqu'une des Rivières, Bayes, rades ou Ports de l'une des deux parties, ils seront reçus et traités avec humanité, et jouiront de toute amitié protection et assistance, et il leur sera permis de se pourvoir de rafraichissemens, de vivres et de toutes choses nécessaires pour leur subsistance, pour la reparation de leurs Vaisseaux, et pour continüer leur voïage, le tout moïennant un prix raisonable, et ils ne seront retenus, en aucune ma-

or hindred from returning out of the said Ports or Roads but may remove and depart when and whither they please without any let or hindrance.

nière ni empêchés de sortir des dits ports ou rades, mais pourront se retirer et partir quand, et comme il leur plaira sans aucun obstacle ni empêchement.

Art. 22.

For the better promoting of Commerce on both Sides, it is agreed that if a War shall break out between the said two Nations, six Months after the Proclamation of War shall be allowed to the Merchants in the Cities and Towns, where they live, for selling and transporting their Goods and Merchandizes; and if any thing be taken from them, or any Injury be done them within that Term by either Party or the People or Subjects of either, full Satisfaction shall be made for the same.

Art. 22.

Afin de promouvoir d'autant mieux le Commerce de deux Côtés, il est convenu que dans le cas où la guerre surviendroit entre les deux Nations susdites, il sera accordé, six mois après la déclaration de guerre, aux marchands dans les Villes et Cités qu'ils habitent, pour rassembler et transporter les marchandises, et s'il en est enlevé quelque chose, ou s'il leur a été fait quelqu'injure durant le terme préscrit ci-dessus, par l'une des deux parties, leurs peuples ou Sujets, il leur sera donné à cet égard pleine et entière satisfaction.

Art. 23.

No Subjects of the most Christian King shall apply for or take any Commission or Letters of marque for arming any Ship or Ships to act as Privateers against the said United States or any of them or against the * Property of any of the Inhabitants of any of them from any Prince or State with which the said United States shall be at War. Nor shall any Citizen Subject or Inhabitant of the said United States or any of them ap-

Art. 23.

Aucun sujet du Roi Très Chretien ne prendra de commission ou de lettres de marque pour armer quelque Vaisseau ou Vaisseaux à l'effet d'agir comme Corsaires contre les dits Etats-unis ou quelques uns d'entr'eux, ou contre les sujets, peuples ou habitans d'iceux, ou contre leur propriété ou celle des habitans d'aucun d'entr'eux, de quelque Prince que ce soit avec lequel les dits Etats-unis seront en guerre. De même aucun Citoïen,

ply for or take any Commission or letters of marque for arming any Ship or Ships to act as Privateers against the Subjects of the most Christian King or any of them or the Property of any of them from any Prince or State with which the said King shall be at War: And if any Person of either Nation shall take such Commissions or Letters of Marque he shall be punished as a Pirate.

* Subjects People or Inhabitants of the said United States or any of them or against the

sujet, ou habitant des susdits Etats-unis et de quelqu'un d'entr' eux ne demandera ni n'acceptera aucune commission ou lettres de marque pour armer quelque Vaisseau, ou Vaisseaux pour courre sus aux sujets de Sa Majesté Très chretienne ou quelques uns d'entre eux ou leur propriété de quelque Prince ou Etat que ce soit avec qui Sa d^{e}. Majesté se trouvera en guerre, et si quelqu'un de l'une ou de l'autre Nation prenoit de pareilles commissions ou lettres de marque il sera puni comme Pirate.

ART. 24.

It shall not be lawful for any foreign Privateers, not belonging to Subjects of the most Christian King nor Citizens of the said United States, who have Commissions from any other Prince or State in enmity with either Nation to fit their Ships in the Ports of either the one or the other of the aforesaid Parties, to sell what they have taken or in any other manner whatsoever to exchange their Ships, Merchandizes or any other lading; neither shall they be allowed even to purchase victuals except such as shall be necessary for their going to the next Port of that Prince or State from which they have Commissions.

ART. 24.

Il ne sera permis à aucun Corsaire étranger non apartenant à quelque sujet de Sa Majesté Très chretienne ou à un Citoïen des dits Etats-unis, lequel aura une commission de la part d'un Prince ou d'une Puissance en guerre avec l'une des deux Nations, d'armer leurs Vaisseaux dans les Ports de l'une des deux parties, ni d'y vendre les prises qu'il aura faites, ni décharger en autre manière quelconque les Vaisseaux, marchandises ou aucune partie de leur Cargaison; Il ne sera même pas permis d'acheter d'autres vivres que ceux qui lui seront nécessaires pour se rendre dans le Port le plus voisin du Prince ou de l'Etat dont il tient sa commission.

Art. 25.

It shall be lawful for all and singular the Subjects of the most Christian King and the Citizens People and Inhabitants of the said United States to sail with their Ships with all manner of Liberty and Security; no distinction being made, who are the Proprietors of the Merchandizes laden thereon, from any Port to the places of those who now are or hereafter shall be at Enmity with the most Christian King or the United States. It shall likewise be Lawful for the Subjects and Inhabitants aforesaid to sail with the Ships and Merchandizes aforementioned and to trade with the same Liberty and security from the Places, Ports and Havens of those who are Enemies of both or either Party without any Opposition or disturbance whatsoever, not only directly from the Places of the Enemy afore mentioned to neutral Places; but also from one Place belonging to an Enemy to another place belonging to an Enemy, whether they be under the Jurisdiction of the same Prince or under several; And it is hereby stipulated that free Ships shall also give a freedom to Goods, and that every thing shall be deemed to be free and exempt, which shall be found on board the Ships belonging to the Subjects of either of the Confederates, although the whole lading or any

Art. 25.

Il sera permis à tous et un chacun des sujets du Roi Très chretien et aux Citoïens, peuple et habitans des susdits Etats-unis de naviguer avec leurs Batimens avec toute liberté et sûreté, sans qu'il puisse être fait d'exception à cet égard, à raison des propriétaires des marchandises chargées sur les dits Batimens venant de quelque Port que ce soit, et destinés pour quelque place d'une Puissance actuellement ennemie ou qui pourra l'être dans la suite de Sa Majesté Très Chretienne ou des Etats-unis. Il sera permis également aux sujets et habitans susmentionnés de naviguer avec leurs Vaisseaux ct mar chandises, et de fréquenter avec la même liberte et sûreté les Places, Ports et havres des Puissances ennemies des deux parties contractantes ou d'une d'entre Elles, sans opposition ni trouble et de faire le Commerce nonseulement directement des Ports de l'ennemi susdit à un port neutre, mais aussi d'un Port ennemi à un autre Port ennemi, soit qu'il se trouve sous sa jurisdiction ou sous celle de plusieurs; Et il est stipulé par le present Traité que les Batimens libres assûreront également la liberté des marchandises, et qu'on jugera libres toutes les choses qui se trouveront àbord des Navires apartenants aux sujets d'une des parties contractantes, quand même le

Part thereof should appertain to the Enemies of either, contraband Goods being always excepted. It is also agreed in like manner that the same Liberty be extended to Persons, who are on board a free Ship, with this Effect, that although they be Enemies to both or either Party, they are not to be taken out of that free Ship, unless they are Soldiers and in actual Service of the Enemies.

chargement ou partie d'icelui apartiendroit aux ennemis de l'une des deux, bien entendu néanmoins que la contrebande sera toujours exceptée. Il est également convenu que cette même liberté s'étendroit aux personnes qui pourroient se trouver àbord du Batiment libre, quand même Elles seroient ennemies de l'une des deux parties contractantes, et Elles ne pourront être enlevées des dits Navires, à moins qu'Elles ne soient militaires, et actuellement au service de l'Ennemi.

ART. 26.

This Liberty of Navigation and Commerce shall extend to all kinds of Merchandizes, excepting those only which are distinguished by the name of contraband; And under this Name of Contraband or prohibited Goods shall be comprehended, Arms, great Guns, Bombs with the fuzes, and other things belonging to them, Cannon Ball, Gun powder, Match, Pikes, Swords, Lances, Spears, halberds, Mortars, Petards, Granades Salt Petre, Muskets, Musket Ball, Bucklers, Helmets, breast Plates, Coats of Mail and the like kinds of Arms proper for arming Soldiers, Musket rests, belts, Horses with their Furniture, and all other Warlike Instruments whatever. These Merchandizes which follow shall not be reckoned among Contraband or prohibited Goods, that

ART. 26.

Cette liberté de navigation et de commerce doit s'étendre sur toutes sortes de marchandises, à l'exception seulement de celles qui sont designées sous le nom de contrebande. Sous ce nom de contrebande ou de marchandises prohibées doivent être compris les armes, Canons, bombes avec leurs fusées et autres choses y relatives, boulets, poudre à tirer, méches, piques, epées, lances, dards, hallebardes, mortiers, petards, grenades, salpêtre, fusils, Balles, Boucliers, Casques, Cuirasses, Cote de mailles et autres armes de cette espèce propres à armer les soldats, portemousqueton, baudriers, chevaux avec leurs Equipages, et tous autres instrumens de guerre quelconques. Les marchandises dénommées ci-après ne seront pas comprises parmi la contrebande ou

is to say, all sorts of Cloths, and all other Manufactures woven of any wool, Flax, Silk, Cotton or any other Materials whatever; all kinds of wearing Apparel together with the Species, whereof they are used to be made; gold & Silver as well coined as uncoin'd, Tin, Iron, Latten, Copper, Brass Coals, as also Wheat and Barley and any other kind of Corn and pulse; Tobacco and likewise all manner of Spices; salted and smoked Flesh, salted Fish, Cheese and Butter, Beer, Oils, Wines, Sugars and all sorts of Salts; & in general all Provisions, which serve for the nourishment of Mankind and the sustenence of Life; furthermore all kinds of Cotton, hemp, Flax, Tar, Pitch, Ropes, Cables, Sails, Sail Cloths, Anchors and any Parts of Anchors; also Ships Masts, Planks, Boards, and Beams of what Trees soever; and all other Things proper either for building or repairing Ships, and all other Goods whatever, which have not been worked into the form of any Instrument or thing prepared for War by Land or by Sea, shall not be reputed Contraband, much less such as have been already wrought and made up for any other Use; all which shall be wholly reckoned among free Goods: * so that they may be transported and carried in the freest manner by the Subjects of both Confederates even to Places belonging to an Enemy

choses prohibées, savoir toutes sortes de draps et toutes autres étoffes de laine, lin, soye, coton ou d'autres matieres quelconques; Toutes sortes de vétemens avec les étoffes dont on a coutume de les faire, l'or et l'argent monnoïé ou non, l'étain, le fer, laiton cuivre, airain, charbons, de même que le froment et l'orge et toute autre sorte de bleds et legumes; Le tabac et toutes les sortes d'épiceries, la viande salée et fumée, poisson sallé, fromage et beurre, bierre, huiles, vins, sucres et toute espece de sel, et en général toutes provisions servant pour la nourriture de l'homme et pour le soutien de la vie; De plus toutes sortes de coton, de chanvre, lin, goudron, poix, cordes, cables, voiles, toiles à voiles, ancres, parties d'ancres, mats, planches, madriers, et bois de toute espèce et toutes autres choses propres à la construction et reparation des Vaisseaux et autres matieres quelconques qui n'ont pas la forme d'un instrument préparé pour la guerre par terre comme par Mer, ne seront pas reputées contrebande, et encore moins celles qui sont déja preparées pour quelqu'autre usage: Toutes les choses dénommées ci-dessus doivent être comprises parmi les marchandises libres de même que toutes les autres marchandises et effets qui ne sont pas compris et particulièrement nommés dans l'énumeration des marchandises de Contrebande;

such Towns or Places being only excepted as are at that time beseiged, blocked up or invested.

* as likewise all other Merchandizes and things, which are not comprehended and particularly mentioned in the foregoing enumeration of contraband Goods:

De manière qu'elles pourront être transportées et conduites de la manière la plus libre par les sujets des deux parties contractantes dans des places ennemies, à l'exception néanmoins de celles qui se trouveroient actuellement assiégées bloquées ou investies.

Art. 27.

To the End that all manner of Dissentions and Quarrels may be avoided and prevented on one Side and the other, it is agreed, that in case either of the Parties hereto should be engaged in War, the Ships and Vessels belonging to the Subjects or People of the other Ally must be furnished with Sea Letters or Passports expressing the name, Property and Bulk of the Ship as also the name and Place of habitation of the Master or Commander of the said Ship, that it may appear thereby, that the Ship really & truely belongs to the Subjects of one of the Parties, which Passport shall be made out and granted according to the Form annexed to this Treaty; they shall likewise be recalled every Year, that is if the Ship happens to return home within the Space of a Year. It is likewise agreed, that such Ships being laden are to be provided not only with Passports as above mentioned, but also with Certificates containing the several Particulars of the Cargo, the Place

Art. 27.

Afin d'écarter et de prévenir de part et d'autre toutes discussions et querelles, il a été convenu que dans le cas où l'une des deux parties se trouveroit engagée dans une guerre, les Vaisseaux et Batimens apartenans aux Sujets ou Peuple de l'autre Allié devront être pourvus de lettres de Mer, ou passeports, les quels exprimeront le nom, la propriété et le port du Navire, ainsi que le nom et la demeure du Maitre ou Commandant du d. Vaisseau, àfin qu'il aparoisse par là que le même vaisseau apartient réellement et véritablement aux sujets de l'une des deux parties contractantes, le quel passeport devra être expédié selon le modèle annexé au present Traité. Ces passeports devront également être renouvellés chaque année dans le cas ou le Vaisseau retourne chez lui dans l'espace d'une année. Il a été convenu également que les Vaisseaux susmentionnés, dans le cas où ils seroient chargés devront être pourvus nonseulement de passeports, mais aussi de Certifi-

whence the Ship sailed and whither she is bound, that so it may be known, whether any forbidden or contraband Goods be on board the same: which Certificates shall be made out by the Officers of the Place, whence the Ship set sail, in the accustomed Form. And if any one shall think it fit or adviseable to express in the said Certificates the Person to whom the Goods on board belong, he may freely do so.

cats contenant le détail de la Cargaison, le lieu d'où le Vaisseau est parti et la déclaration des marchandises de Contrebande qui pourroient se trouver àbord; Lesquels Certificats devront être expédiés dans la forme accoutumée par les officiers du lieu d'où le Vaisseau aura fait voile, Et s'il étoit jugé utile ou prudent d'exprimer dans les dits passeports la personne à laquelle les marchandises apartiennent, on pourra le faire librement.

Art. 28.

The Ships of the Subjects and Inhabitants of either of the Parties, coming upon any Coasts belonging to either of the said Allies, but not willing to enter into Port, or being entred into Port and not willing to unload their Cargoes or break Bulk, they shall be treated according to the general Rules prescribed or to be prescribed relative to the Object in Question.

Art. 28.

Dans le cas ou les Vaisseaux des sujets et habitans de l'une des deux parties contractantes aprocheroient des côtes de l'autre, sans cependant avoir le dessein d'entrer dans le port, ou après être entré, sans avoir le dessein de décharger la Cargaison ou rompre leur charge, on se conduira à leur égard suivant les réglemens généraux préscrits ou à prescrire relativement à l'objet dont il est question.

Art. 29.

If the Ships of the said Subjects, People or Inhabitants of either of the Parties shall be met with either sailing along the Coasts or on the high Seas by any Ship of War of the other or by any Privateers, the said Ships of War or Privateers, for the avoiding of any Disorder shall remain out of Can-

Art. 29.

Lorsqu'un Batiment apartenant aux dits sujets, peuple et habitans de l'une des deux parties, sera rencontré navigant le long des Côtes ou en pleine Mer par un vaisseau de guerre de l'autre, ou par un Armateur, le dit Vaisseau de guerre ou Armateur, âfin d'éviter tout désordre, se tiendra hors de la portée

non Shot, and may send their Boats aboard the Merchant Ship, which they shall so meet with, and may enter her to number of two or three Men only to whom the Master or Commander of such Ship or Vessel shall exhibit his passport concerning the Property of the Ship made out according to the Form inserted in this present Treaty, and the Ship, when she shall have shewed such Passport shall be free and at Liberty to pursue her Voyage, so as it shall not be lawful to molest or search her in any manner or to give her chase, or force her to quit her intended Course.

du Canon, et pourra envoïer sa Chaloupe àbord du Batiment marchand et y faire entrer deux ou trois hommes auxquels le Maitre ou Commandant du Batiment montrera son passeport, lequel devra être conforme à la formule annexée au present Traité, et constatera la propriété du Batiment, et après que le dit Batiment aura exhibé un pareil passeport, il lui sera libre de continüer son voïage, et il ne sera pas permis de le molester ni de chercher, en aucune manière, de lui donner la chasse ou de le forcer de quiter la Course qu'il s'étoit proposée.

ART. 30.

It is also agreed that all Goods, when once put on board the Ships or Vessels of either of the two contracting Parties shall be subject to no farther Visitation; but all Visitation or Search shall be made before hand, and all prohibited Goods shall be stopped on the Spot, before the same be put on board, unless there are manifest Tokens or Proofs of fraudulent Practice: nor shall either the Persons or goods of the Subjects of his most Christian Majesty or the United States be put under any arrest or molested by any other kind of Embargo for that Cause; and only the Subject of that State, to whom the said Goods have been or shall be prohibited and who shall presume

ART. 30.

Il est convenu que lorsque les marchandises auront été chargées sur les Vaisseaux ou Batimens de l'une des deux parties contractantes, elles ne pourront plus être assujeties à aucune visite; Toute visite et recherche devant être faite avant le chargement, et les marchandises prohibées devant être arrêtées et saisies sur la plage avant de pouvoir être embarquées, à moins qu'on n'ait des indices manifestes ou des preuves de versements frauduleux. De même aucun des sujets de Sa Majesté Très Chretienne ou des Etats-unis, ni leurs marchandises ne pourront être arrêtés ni molestés pour cette cause par aucune espèce d'embargo; Et les seuls sujets de l'Etat, auxquels

to sell or alienate such sort of Goods shall be duly punished for the Offence.

les d[es]. marchandises auront été prohibées, et qui se seront emancipés à vendre et aliéner de pareilles marchandises, seront düement punis pour cette contravention.

ART. 31.

The two contracting Parties grant mutually the Liberty of having each in the Ports of the other, Consuls, Vice Consuls, Agents and Commissaries, whose Functions shall be regulated by a particular Agreement.

ART. 31.

Les deux parties contractantes se sont accordées mutuellement la faculté de tenir dans leurs ports respectifs des Consuls, Vice-Consuls, Agents et Commissaires, dont les fonctions seront reglées par une Convention particulière.

ART. 32.

And the more to favour and facilitate the Commerce which the Subjects of the United States may have with France, the most Christian King will grant them in Europe one or more free Ports, where they may bring and dispose of all the Produce and Merchandize of the thirteen United States; and his Majesty will also continue to the Subjects of the said States, the free Ports which have been and are open in the french Islands of America. Of all which free Ports, the said Subjects of the United States shall enjoy the Use, agreable to the Regulations which relate to them.

ART. 32.

Pour d'autant plus favoriser et faciliter le Commerce que les sujets des Etats-unis feront avec la France, le Roi Très Chretien leur accordera en Europe un ou plusieurs ports francs dans lesquels ils pourront amener et débiter toutes les denrées et marchandises provenant des treize Etats-unis; Sa Majesté conservera d'un autre côté aux sujets des dits Etats les ports francs qui ont été et sont ouverts dans les Isles françoises de l'Amerique. De tous les quels Ports francs les dits sujets des Etats-unis jouiront conformement aux règlemens qui en déterminent l'usage.

ART. 33.

The present Treaty shall be ratified on both Sides and the Ratifi-

ART. 33.

Le present Traité sera ratifié de part et d'autre et les ratifications

cations shall be exchanged in the Space of Six Months, or sooner if possible.

seront echangées dans l'espace de six mois ou plustôt si faire se peut.

In Faith whereof, the respective Plenipotentiaries have signed the above Articles, both in the French and English Languages, declaring nevertheless that the present Treaty was originally composed and concluded in the French Language, and they have thereto affixed their Seals.

En foi de quoi les Plenipotentiaires respectifs ont signé les articles ci-dessus tant en langue Françoise qu'en langue Angloise; Déclarant néanmoins que le present Traité a eté originairement redigé et arrêté en langue françoise; Et Ils y ont apposé le cachet de leurs armes.

Done at Paris this Sixth Day of February, one thousand seven hundred & seventy eight.

Fait à Paris le sixieme jour du mois de fevrier mil sept cent soixante dixhuit.

C. A. Gerard [seal] B. Franklin [seal] Silas Deane [seal] Arthur Lee [seal]

Note.—The English translation is in the writing of William Temple Franklin.—W. C. F.

Form of the Passports and Letters, which are to be given to the Ships and Barks, according to the twenty seventh Article of this Treaty.

To all who shall see these Presents greeting: It is hereby made known that leave and Permission has been given to .... Master and Commander of the Ship called ...... of the town of .... burthen .... Tons or thereabouts lying at present in the Port and Haven of .... and bound for .... & laden with

Forme des passeports et lettres qui doivent être donnés aux Vaisseaux et Barques conformement à l'Article vingt sept du Traité cidessus.

A Tous Ceux qui les presentes verront, soit notoire que faculté et permission a été accordée à .... Maitre ou Commandant du Navire appellé .... de la ville de .... de la capacite de .... Tonneaux ou environ, se trouvant presentement dans le Port et Havre de .... et destiné pour .... chargé de ....

. . . . after that his Ship has been visited and before sailing he shall make Oath before the Officers, who have the Jurisdiction of Maritime Affairs, that the said Ship belongs to one or more of the [subjects of . . . .] citizens of U. S. of A.[1] the Act whereof shall be put at the End of these presents, as likewise that he will keep and cause to be kept by his Crew on board, the Marine Ordinances and Regulations, and enter in the proper Office a List signed and witnessed containing the Names and Sirnames, the Places of Birth and abode of the Crew of his Ship and of all who shall embark on board her, whom he shall not take on board without the Knowledge and permission of the Officers of the Marine; and in every Port or Haven, where he shall enter with his Ship he shall shew this present Leave to the Officers & Judges of the Marine, and shall give a faithful Account to them of what passed and was done during his Voyage, and he shall carry the Colours, Arms and Ensigns of the (King, or United States) during his Voyage. In witness whereof we have signed these Presents and put the Seal of our Arms thereunto, and caused the same to be countersigned by . . . . . . at . . . . . . the . . . . . . Day of . . . . . . AD. . . . .

[1] Corrected in another hand.

qu'après que son Navire a été visité, et avant son départ, il prêtera serment entre les mains des Officiers de Marine, que le d. Navire apartient à un ou plusieurs [sujets de . . . .] citoïens des etats unis d'Amerique [1] dont l'acte sera mis à la fin des présentes; de même qu'il gardera et fera garder par son Equipage les ordonnances et réglements maritimes, et remettra une liste signée et confirmée par Temoins, contenant les noms et surnoms, les lieux de naissance et la demeure des personnes composant l'équipage de son Navire et de tous ceux qui s'y embarqueront, lesquels il ne recevra pas àbord sans la connoissance et la permission des Officiers de Marine; Et dans chaque Port ou havre où il entrera avec son Navire, il montrera la presente permission aux Officiers et Juges de Marine et leur fera un raport fidèle de ce qui s'est passé durant son voïage, et il portera les couleurs, armes et enseignes du (Roi ou des Etats unis) durant son dit voïage. En temoin de quoi Nous avons signé les presentes, les avons fait contresigner par . . . . . . et y avons fait apposer le sceau de nos armes.

Donné . . . . le . . . . de l'an de grace le . . . . . .

[1] Corrected in another hand.

TREATY OF ALLIANCE, EVENTUAL AND DEFENSIVE.

LEWIS, by the grace of God king of France and Navarre—To all who shall see these presents, Greeting.

The Congress of the United States of America having, by their plenipotentiaries residing in France, proposed to form with us a defensive and eventual alliance; and willing to give the said states an efficacious proof of the interest we take in their prosperity, we have determined to conclude the said alliance. For these causes, and other good considerations us thereunto moving, we, reposing entire confidence in the abilities and experience, zeal and fidelity for our service, of our dear and beloved Conrad Alexander Gérard, royal syndic of the city of Strasburg, secretary of our council of state, have nominated, commissioned and deputed, and by these presents signed with our hand, do nominate, commission and depute him our plenipotentiary, giving him power and special command to act in this quality, and confer, negotiate, treat and agree conjointly with the abovementioned

LOUIS par la grâce de Dieu, Roy de France et de Navarre à tous ceux qui ses présentes lettres verront, SALUT.

Le Congrès des États-Unis de l'Amériquc septentrionale nous ayant fait proposer par ses plénipotentiaires résidans en France de former avec nous une alliance défensive et éventuelle, et voulant donner aux dits États-unis une preuve efficace de l'intérêt que nous prenons à leur prosperité, nous nous sommes déterminé à conclure la dite Alliance. A CES CAUSES, et autres bonnes considérations à ce nous mouvant, nous confiant entièrement en la capacité et expérience, zèle et fidélité pour notre service de notre cher et ame Conrad Alexander Gérard Sindic royal de la ville de Strasbourg, secrétaire de notre conseil d'État, nous l'avons nommé, commis et deputé, et par ces présentes signées de notre main, le nommons, committons, et députons notre plénipotentiaire lui donnant pouvoir et mandement spécial d'agir en cette qualité, et de conferer, négocier, traiter et convenir

plenipotentiaries of the United States, vested in like manner with powers in due form, to determine and conclude such articles, conditions, conventions, declarations, definitive treaty, and any other acts whatever, as he shall judge proper to answer the end which we propose; promising, on the faith and word of a king, to agree to, confirm and establish for ever, to accomplish and execute punctually whatever our said beloved Conrad Alexander Gérard shall have stipulated and signed, in virtue of the present power, without ever contravening it, or suffering it to be contravened, for any cause and under any pretext whatever; as likewise to cause our letters of ratification to be made in due form, and to have them in order, or to be exchanged at the time that shall be agreed upon. For such is our pleasure.

In testimony whereof we have set our seal to these presents.

Given at Versailles, the thirteenth day of January, in the year of grace, one thousand seven hundred and seventy-eight.

[L. S.] LOUIS.

By the King.

GRAVIER DE VERGENNES.

conjoinctement avec les sus-dits Plénipotentiaires des États-unis revêtus également de pouvoirs en bonne forme arrêter, conclure, et signer tels articles, conditions, conventions, déclarations, Traité définitif et autres Actes quelconques qu'il jugera convenables pour remplir le but, que nous nous proposons. Promettant, en foi de parole de Roi, d'avoir agréable, tenir ferme et stable à toujours, accomplir et exécuter ponctuellement tout ce que notre dit cher et amé Conrad Alexander Gérard aura stipulé et signé en vertu du présent pouvoir, sans jamais y contrevenir, ni permettre qu'il y soit contrevenu, pour quelque cause, et sous quelque prétexte que ce puisse être, comme aussi d'en faire expédier nos lettres de ratification en bonne forme, et de les faire délivrer pour être échangées dans le temps, dont il sera convenu. CAR TEL EST NOTRE PLAISIR. En témoin de quoi nous avons fait mettre notre Scel à ces présentes. Donné à Versailles le trentième jour du mois de Janvier l'an de grace mil sept cent soixante et dix huit, et de notre regne le quatrième.

LOUIS

Par le Roi

[L. S.] GRAVIER DE VERGENNES [1]

[1] Copies of these powers are in the Department of State in the writing of Benjamin Franklin and William Temple Franklin. W. C. F.

TREATY OF ALLIANCE.

The most Christian King and the United States of North America, to wit, Newhampshire, Massachusetts Bay, Rhodes island, Connecticut, Newyork, New Jersey, Pennsylvania, Delaware, Maryland, Virginia, North Carolina, South Carolina, and Georgia, having this Day concluded a Treaty of amity and Commerce, for the réciprocal advantage of their Subjects and Citizens have thought it necessary to take into considération the means of Strengthening those engagements and of rendring them useful to the safety and tranquility of the two parties, particularly in case Great Britain in Resentment of that connection and of the good correspondence which is the object of the Said Treaty should break the Peace with france, either by direct hostilities, or by hindring her commerce and navigation, in a manner contrary to the Rights of Nations, and the Peace Subsisting between the two Crowns; and his Majesty and the Said united States having resolved in that Case to join their Councils and efforts against the Enterprises of their common Enemy, the respective Plenipotentiaries, impower'd to concert the Clauses & conditions proper to fulfil the said Intentions, have, after the most mature Deliberation, concluded and determined on the following Articles.

TRAITÉ D'ALLIANCE ÉVENTUELLE ET DÉFFENSIVE.

Le Roi Très Chrétien et les Etats-unis de l'Amerique septentrionale, savoir New-hampshire, la Baye de Massachusset, Rhode-Island Connecticut, Newyork, New-Jersey, Pensylvanie, Delaware, Maryland, Virginie, Caroline septentrionale, Caroline Meridionale et Georgie; ayant conclu ce jourd'huy un Traité d'Amitié, de bonne intelligence et de commerce, pour l'avantage réciproque de leurs Sujets et Citoyens, ils ont cru devoir prendre en considération les moyens de resserrer leurs liaisons, et de les rendre utiles à la sureté et à la tranquilité des deux Parties, notament dans le cas où la Grande Bretagne, en haine de ces mêmes liaisons et de la bonne correspondance qui forment l'objet du dit Traité, se porteroit à rompre la paix avec la france, soit en l'attaquant hostilement, soit en troublant son commerce et sa navigation, d'une maniere contraire au droit des gens et à la paix subsistante entre les deux Couronnes; Et Sa Majesté et les dits Etats-unis ayant résolu éventuellement d'unir, dans le cas prévû, leurs conseils et leurs efforts contre les entreprises de leur ennemi commun, les Plenipotentiaires respectifs, chargés de concerter les clauses et conditions propres à remplir leurs intentions, ont, après la plus mure délibération, conclu et arresté les points et articles qui s'ensuivent.

Art. 1.

If war should break out between france and Great Britain, during the continuence of the present war between the united States and England, his Majesty and the said united States, shall make it a common cause, and aid each other mutually with their good Offices their Counsels, and their forces, according to the exigence of Conjunctures as becomes good & faithful Allies.

Article premier.

Si la guerre éclate entre la france et la Grande Brétagne, pendant la durée de la guerre actuelle entre les Etats-unis et l'Angleterre, Sa Majesté et les dits Etats-unis feront cause commune et s'entr'aideront mutuellement de leurs bons offices, de leurs conseils et de leurs forces, selon l'exigence des conjonctures, ainsy qu'il convient à de bons et fideles Alliés.

Art. 2.

The essential and direct End of the present defensive alliance is to maintain effectually the liberty, Sovereignty, and independance absolute and unlimited of the said united States, as well in Matters of Gouvernement as of commerce.

Article second.

Le but essentiel et direct de la présente alliance deffensive, est de maintenir efficacement la liberté, la souveraineté, et l'indépendance absolue et illimitée des dits Etats unis, tant en matiére politique que de commerce.

Art. 3.

The two contracting Parties shall each on its own Part, and in the manner it may judge most proper, make all the efforts in its Power, against their common Ennemy in order to attain the end proposed.

Article trois.

Les deux Parties contractantes feront chacune de leur côté, et de la maniére qu'elles jugeront plus convenable, tous les efforts, qui seront en leur pouvoir, contre leur ennemi commun, afin d'atteindre au but qu'elles se proposent.

Art. 4.

The contracting Parties agree that in case either of them should form any particular Enterprise in which the concurrence of the other may be desired, the Party whose concurrence is desired shall readily,

Article quatre.

Les Parties contractantes sont convenues que dans le cas où l'une d'entre Elles formeroit quelqu'entreprise particuliére, pour laquelle elle désireroit le concours de l'autre, celle ci, se prêteroit de bonne

and with good faith, join to act in concert for that Purpose, as far as circumstances and its own particular Situation will permit; and in that case, they shall regulate by a particular Convention the quantity and kind of Succour to be furnished, and the Time and manner of its being brought into action, as well as the advantages which are to be its Compensation.

foi à un concert sur cet objet, autant que les circonstances et sa propre situation pourront le lui permettre, [et dans ce cas, on reglera par une Convention particuliére la portée des secours à fournir, et le tems et la maniére de le faire agir, ainsy que les avantages destinés à en former la compensation.

ART. 5.

If the united States Should think fit to attempt the Reduction of the British Power remaining in the Northern Parts of America, or the Islands of Bermudas, those Contries or Islands in case of Success, shall be confederated with or dependant upon the said united States.

ARTICLE CINQ.

Si les Etats-unis jugent à propos de tenter la reduction des Isles Bermudes et des parties septentrionales de l'Amérique qui sont encore au pouvoir de la Grande Bretagne, les dites Isles et Contrées, en cas de succès, entreront dans la confedération ou seront dépendantes des dits Etats-unis.

ART. 6.

The Most Christian King renounces for ever the possession of the Islands of Bermudas as well as of any part of the continent of North america which before the treaty of Paris in 1763, or in virtue of that Treaty, were acknowledged to belong to the Crown of Great Britain, or to the united States heretofore called British Colonies, or which are at this Time or have lately been under the Power of The King and Crown of Great Britain.

ARTICLE SIX.

Le Roi très Chrétien renonce à posseder jamais les Bermudes ni aucune des parties du Continent de l'Amérique septentrionalle qui, avant le Traité de Paris de mil sept cent soixante trois, ou en vertu de ce Traité, ont été reconnuës appartenir à la Couronne de la Grande Bretagne ou aux Etats-unis, qu'on appelloit ci devant Colonies Britanniques, ou qui sont maintenant ou ont été récemment sous la jurisdiction et sous le pouvoir de la Couronne de la Grande Bretagne.

Art. 7.

If his most Christian Majesty Shall think proper to attack any of the Islands situated in the Gulph of Mexico, or near that Gulph, which are at present under the Power of Great Britain, all the said Isles, in case of success, shall appertain to the Crown of france.

Article sept.

Si Sa Majesté Très Chrétienne juge à propos d'attaquer aucune des Isles situées dans le Golphe de Méxique ou près du dit Golphe, qui sont actuellement au pouvoir de la Grande Bretagne, toutes les dites Isles, en cas de succès, appartiendront à la Couronne de France.

Art. 8.

Neither of the two Parties Shall conclude either Truce or Peace with Great Britain, without the formal consent of the other first obtain'd; and they mutually engage not to lay down their arms, until the Independence of the united States Shall have been formally or tacitly assured by the Treaty or Treaties that shall terminate the War.

Article huit.

Aucune des deux Parties ne pourra conclure ni treve ni paix avec la Grande Brétagne, sans le consentement préalable et formel de l'autre Partie, et Elles s'engagent mutuellement à ne mettre bas les armes, que lorsque l'indépendance des dits Etats-unis aura été assurée formellement ou tacitement par le Traité ou les Traités qui termineront la guerre.

Art. 9.

The contracting Parties declare, that being resolved to fulfil each on its own Part the clauses and conditions of the present Treaty of alliance, according to its own power and circumstances, there Shall be no after claim of compensation on one side or the other whatever may be the event of the War.

Article neuf.

Les Parties contractantes déclarent, qu'etant resolues de remplir chacune de son côté les clauses et conditions du présent Traité d'alliance selon son pouvoir et les circonstances, Elles n'auront aucune repetition, ni aucun dedommagement à se demander réciproquement, quelque puisse etre l'evenement de la guerre.

ART. 10.

The most Christian King and the United States, agree to invite or admit other Powers who may have received injuries from England to make common cause with them, and to accede to the present alliance, under such conditions as shall be freely agreed to and settled between all the Parties.

ARTICLE DIX.

Le Roi Très Chretien et les Etats-unis sont convenus d'inviter de concert ou d'admettre les Puissances, qui auront des griefs contre l'Angleterre, à faire cause commune avec Eux, et à accéder à la présente alliance, sous les conditions qui seront librement agrées et convenuës entre toutes les Parties.

ART. 11.

The two Parties guarantee mutually from the present time and forever, against all other powers, to wit, the united States to his most Christian Majesty the present Possessions of the Crown of france in America as well as those which it may acquire by the future Treaty of peace: and his most Christian Majesty guarantees on his part to the united states, their liberty, Sovereignty, and Independence absolute, and unlimited, as well in Matters of Government as commerce and also their Possessions, and the additions or conquests that their Confedération may obtain during the war, from any of the Dominions now or heretofore possessed by Great Britain in North america, conformable to the 5th. & 6th articles above written, the whole as their Possessions shall be fixed and assured to the said States at the moment of the cessation of their present War with England.

ARTICLE ONZE.

Les deux Parties se garantissent mutuellement dès à present et pour toujours envers et contre tous, Savoir, les Etats-unis à Sa Majesté très Chrétienne les possessions actuelles de la Couronne de France en Amérique, ainsy que celles qu' Elle pourra acquérir par le futur Traité de paix; Et Sa Majesté Trés Chretienne, garantit de son côté aux Etats-unis leur liberté, leur souveraineté et leur indépendance absolue et illimitée, tant en matiére de politique que de commerce, ainsy que leurs possessions et les accroissements ou conquêtes que leur confédération pourra se procurer pendant la guerre, d'aucun des Domaines maintenant ou cidevant possedés par la Grande Bretagne dans l'Amérique septentrionale, conformément aux articles cinq et six ci dessus, et tout ainsy que leurs possessions seront fixées et assurées aux dits Etats, au moment de la cessation de leur guerre actuelle contre l'Angleterre.

ART. 12.

In order to fix more precisely the sense and application of the preceding article, the Contracting Parties declare, that in case of a rupture between france and England, the reciprocal Guarantee, declared in the said article shall have its full force and effect the moment Such War shall break out; and if such rupture shall not take place, the mutual obligations of the said guarantee shall not commence, until the moment of the cessation of the present War between the united states and England Shall have ascertained their Possessions.

ARTICLE DOUZE.

Affin de fixer plus précisément le sens et l'application de l'article précédent, les Parties contractantes déclarent qu'en cas de rupture entre la france et l'Angleterre, la garantie réciproque enoncée dans le sus dit article, aura toute sa force et valeur du moment où la guerre éclatera, et si la rupture n'avoit pas lieu, les obligations mutuelles de la ditte garantie, ne commenceroient, que du moment sus dit, où la cessation de la guerre actuelle entre les Etats unis et l'Angleterre, aura fixé leurs possessions.

ART. 13.

The present Treaty Shall be ratified on both sides and the Ratifications shall be exchanged in the space of six months, or sooner if possible.

ARTICLE TREIZE.

Le present Traité sera ratiffié de part et d'autre et les ratiffications seront échangées dans l'espace de six mois ou plustôt, si faire se peut.

IN FAITH where of the respective Plenipotentiaries, to wit on the part of the most Christian King Conrad Alexander Gerard royal syndic of the City of Strasbourgh & Secretary of his Majestys Council of State and on the part of the United States Benjamin Franklin Deputy to the General Congress from the State of Pensylvania and President of the Convention of the same state, Silas Deane heretofore Deputy

EN FOI de quoi les Plenipotentiaires respectifs savoir de la part du Roi Très Chretien le S[r]. Conrad, Alexandre Gerard Sindic royal de la ville de Strasbourg et Sécrétaire du Conseil d'Etat de Sa Majesté, et de la part des Etats-unis les S[rs]. Benjamin franklin Deputé au Congrès général de la part de l'Etat de Peñsylvanie et President de la Convention du meme Etat, Siles Deane Cy devant Député de l'Etat de Connecticut et

from the State of Connecticut & Arthur Lee Councellor at Law have signed the above Articles both in the French and English Languages, declaring Nevertheless that the present Treaty was originally composed and concluded in the French Language, and they have hereunto affixed their Seals.

Done at Paris, this Sixth Day of February, one thousand seven hundred and seventy eight.

Arthur Leé *Conseiller ès loix* ont signé les articles ci dessus, tant en langue françoise qu'en langue Angloise, déclarant néanmoins que le present Traité, a êté originairement redigé et arrêté en langue françoise, et ils les ont munis du cachet de leurs armes.

Fait à Paris le sixieme jour du mois de fevrier mil sept cent soixante dixhuit.[1]

C. A. Gerard	B. Franklin	Silas Deane	Arthur Lee
[seal]	[seal]	[seal]	[seal]

[1] These words are in the writing of Gérard. W. C. F.

ACT SEPARATE AND SECRET.

ACT SEPARATE AND SECRET.

The most Christian King declares in consequence of the intimate union which Subsists between him and the King of Spain, that in concluding with the united States of America this Treaty of amity and commerce, and that of eventual and defensive alliance, his Majesty hath intended and intends to reserve expressly, as he reserves by this present separate and secret act, to his said Catholick Majesty, the Power of acceding to the Said Treatys, and to participate in their stipulations at such time as he shall judge proper. It being well understood nevertheless, that if any of the Stipulations of the Said Treatys are not agreable to the King of Spain, his Catholick Majesty may propose other conditions analogous to the principal aim of the alliance and conformable to the Rules of equality, reciprocity & friendship.

The Deputies of the united States in the name of their constituents, accept the present Declaration in its full extent, and the Deputy of the said States who is fully impowerd to treat with Spain, promises to sign on the first Requisition of his Catholic Majesty, the act or acts necessary to

ACTE SÉPARÉ ET SECRET.

Le Roi très Chrétien déclare en conséquence de l'union intime qui subsiste entre lui et le Roi d'Espagne, qu'en concluant avec les Etats-unis de l'Amérique septentrionale le traité d'amitié et de commerce et celui d'alliance eventuelle et deffensive, Sa Majesté a entendu et entend reserver expressement, comme elle reserve par le présent acte séparé et secret à Sa dite Majesté Catholique la faculté d'acceder auxdits Traités, et de participer à Leurs stipulations, dans quelque tems qu'Elle le juge à propos, bien entendu néanmoins que si quelques unes des stipulations des dits Traités ne convenoient point au Roi d'Espagne, Sa Majesté Catholique seroit maitresse de proposed d'autres conditions analogues au but principal de l'Alliance, et conformes aux loix de l'égalité, de la réciprocité et de l'amitié.

Les Députés des Etats-unis au nom de leurs commettans acceptent la présente Déclaration dans toute son étendue, et le Député des dits Etats spécialement chargé des pleinpouvoirs, pour traiter avec la Couronne d'Espagne, promet de signer à la premiére réquisition de Sa Majesté Catholique l'acte ou les

communicate to him the Stipulations of the Treaties above written; and the said Deputy shall endeavour in good faith the adjustment of the points in which the King of spain may propose any alteration, conformable to the principles of equality, reciprocity and the most sincere and perfect amity; [1] he the said Deputy not doubting but that the Person or Persons impower'd by his Catholic Majesty to treat with the United States will do the same with regard to any Alterations of the same kind that may be thought necessary by the said Plenipotentiary of the United States. In Faith whereof the respective Plenipotentiaries have signed the present separate and secret Article, and affixed to the same their Seals.

Done at Paris, this sixth Day of February, one thousand seven hundred and seventy-eight.[2]

C. A. GERARD [SEAL]   B FRANKLIN [SEAL]

actes nécessaires, pour lui rendre communes les stipulations des Traités ci dessus relatés, et le dit Député se prêtera de bonne foi à l'ajustement des points auxquels le Roi d'Espagne voudroit apporter quelques changemens, conformément aux principes de l'égalité de la réciprocité et de l'amitié la plus parfaite et la plus sincére, ne doutant pas le dit Député que la personne ou les personnes qui seront autorisées par le Roi Catholique à traiter avec les Etats unis, n'en usent de même, relativement aux changemens de la même nature que le dit Plenipotentiaire des Etats unis pourra juger nécessaires.

En foi de quoi les Plénipotentiaires respectifs ont signé le présent article separé et secret, et y ont apposé le cachet de leurs armes.

Fait à Paris le sixieme jour du mois de fevrier mil sept cent soixante dixhuit.[1]

SILAS DEANE
[SEAL]

ARTHUR LEE Deputé plenipotentiaire pour la France et l'Espagne.
[SEAL]

[1] From this point to the word *Seals* the writing is that of William Temple Franklin. W. C. F.

[2] These words are in the writing of Benjamin Franklin. W. C. F.

[1] These words were written by Gérard. W. C. F.

or sooner if possible.

In faith whereof the respective Plenipotentiaries, to wit on the part of the most Christian King Conrad Alexander Gerard royal Syndic of the City of Strasbourgh & Secretary of his Majesty's Council of State and on the part of the United States Benjamin Franklin Deputy to the General Congress from the State of Pensylvania and President of the Convention of the same state, Silas Deane heretofore Deputy from the State of Connecticut & Arthur Lee Counsellor at Law have signed the above Articles both in the French and English Languages declaring Nevertheless that the present Treaty was originally composed and concluded in the French Language, and they have hereunto affixed their Seals

Done at Paris, this Sixth Day of February, one thousand seven hundred and seventy eight.

C. A. Gerard B Franklin

Six mois ou plutôt, si faire se peut.

En foi de quoi les Plenipotentiaires respectifs, savoir de la part du Roi Tres Chretien le Sr. Conrad, Alexandre Gerard Sindic royal de la ville de Strasbourg et Secretaire du Conseil d'Etat de Sa Majesté, et de la part des Etats unis les Srs. Benjamin Franklin Deputé au Congrès général de la part de l'Etat de Pensylvanie et President de la Convention du meme Etat, Silas Deane cy devant Deputé de l'Etat de Connecticut et Arthur Lée Conseiller ès loix ont signé les articles ci dessus, tant en langue françoise qu'en langue Angloise, déclarant néanmoins que le present traité a été originairement redigé et arrêté en langue françoise, et ils les ont munis du cachet de leurs armes.

Fait à Paris le sixieme jour du mois de fevrier mil sept cent soixante dix huit.

Silas Deane Arthur Lee

THE LAST PAGE OF THE TREATY OF ALLIANCE REPRODUCED FROM THE ORIGINAL IN THE DEPARTMENT OF STATE

III
THE RATIFICATION

THE RATIFICATION.

JOURNALS OF CONGRESS.

SATURDAY, MAY 2, 1778

. . . .

Adjourned to 10 o'Clock on Monday.

During the adjournment, Mr. [Simeon] Deane, brother to S[ilas] Deane, Esq[r] one of the commissioners at the court of Versailles, arrived express from France, with sundry important despatches; Whereupon,

Congress was convened, and the despatches laid before them. Among which a treaty of commerce and alliance, concluded between the king of France and the United States of America, on the 6 February last.

MONDAY, MAY 4, 1778

Congress took into consideration the treaties concluded between the king of France and the United States of America, and after some time spent thereon, adjourned to 3 o'Clock.

THREE O'CLOCK, P. M.

Congress resumed the consideration of the treaty of amity and commerce concluded at Paris, on the 6th of February, between the most Christian king and the United States of America, and signed by Conrad Alexander Gérard, plenipotentiary, on the part of his most Christian Majesty, and Benjamin Franklin, Silas Deane and Arthur Lee, plenipotentiaries on the part of the United States of America, and the same being read, duly weighed and considered.

Resolved unanimously, That the same be and is hereby ratified.

Congress also took into consideration the treaty of Alliance, concluded at Paris on the 6 day of February, 1778, between the most Christian King and the United States of America, and signed by Conrad Alexander Gérard, plenipotentiary on the part of his most Christian Majesty, and Benjamin Franklin, Silas Deane, and Arthur Lee, plenipotentiaries on the part of the United States of America, and the same being read, duly weighed and considered.

Resolved, unanimously, That the same be and is hereby ratified.

Congress also took into consideration an "Act separate and secret", concluded at Paris, the 6 day of February, 1778, between his most Christian Majesty and the United States of America, signed as the above, and the same being duly weighed,

Resolved, unanimously, That the same be, and is hereby ratified.

Resolved, That this Congress entertain the highest sense of the magnanimity and wisdom of his most Christian majesty, so strongly exemplified in the treaty of amity and commerce, and the treaty of alliance, entered into on the part of his majesty, with these United States, at Paris, on the 6th day of February last; and the commissioners, or any of them, representing these States at the court of France, are directed to present the grateful acknowledgments of this Congress to his most Christian majesty, for his truly magnanimous conduct respecting these states, in the said generous and disinterested treaties, and to assure his majesty, on the part of this Congress, it is sincerely wished that the friendship so happily commenced between France and these United States may be perpetual.

Resolved, That a committee of three be appointed to prepare the form of ratification of the foregoing treaties:

The members chosen, Mr. R[ichard] H[enry] Lee, Mr. [Francis] Dana, and Mr. [William Henry] Drayton.

||Adjourned to 10 o'Clock to Morrow.||

TUESDAY, MAY 5, 1778

. . . .

Resolved, That the commissioners, or any one of them, representing these states at the court of France, be instructed to inform that court that, although Congress have readily ratified the treaties of amity and commerce, and treaty of alliance, and the act, separate and secret, between his most Christian majesty and these United States, in order to evince more clearly their sense of the magnanimity and goodness of his most Christian majesty, evidenced in the said treaties; yet, ~~Congress are of opinion that dissentions may hereafter arise from the imposition of duties upon the exportation of the produce and manufactures of the dominions of his most Christian Majesty to these states, whilst similar duties on the produce of these states might be prevented by means of the prohibition contained in the 12 Article of the said treaty; wherefore relying on the same magnanimity and desire of permanent friendship and mutual advantage between the two countries which have strongly marked the councils of France in this treaty, and sincerely desirous of establishing the most permanent and perpetual friendship and alliance founded on equal interest and convenience have no doubt but that it will be agreed that the~~ from a sincere desire of rendering the friendship and alliance, so happily begun, permanent and perpetual, and being apprehensive that differences may arise from the 11 and 12 articles in the treaty of amity and commerce, Congress are desirous that the said 11 and 12 articles may be revoked and utterly expunged:

The commissioners, or any of them, are therefore instructed to use their best endeavours to procure the abolition of the said 11 and 12 articles of the said treaty.

Massachusetts bay,
~~Mr. Lovell,~~ ay
~~Dana,~~ ay } *
Rhode Island,
~~Mr. Ellery,~~ no } no
Connecticut,
~~Mr. Sherman,~~ ay
~~Huntington,~~ ay
~~Wolcott,~~ ay } ay
New York,
~~Mr. Livingston,~~ ay
~~Morris,~~ ay } ay
New Jersey,
~~Mr. Scudder,~~ ay } ay
Pensylvania,
~~Mr. James Smith,~~ no
~~J. B. Smith,~~ no
~~Clingan,~~ ay } no
Maryland,
~~Mr. Chase,~~ ay
~~Carroll,~~ ay
~~Henry,~~ ay
~~Plater,~~ ay } ay
Virginia,
~~Mr. R. H. Lee,~~ ay
~~F. L. Lee,~~ ay
~~Adams,~~ ay } ay
South Carolina,
~~Mr. Laurens,~~ ay
~~Drayton,~~ ay
~~Hutson,~~ ay
~~Mathews,~~ ay } ay
Georgia,
~~Mr. Langworthy,~~ ay } ay

The committee appointed to prepare the form of a ratification, brought in the same, which was read and agreed to:

The Congress of the United States of New Hampshire, Massachusetts Bay, Rhode Island and Providence Plantations, Connecticut, New York, New Jersey, Pennsylvania, Delaware, Maryland, Virginia, North Carolina, South Carolina, and Georgia, by the grace of God, sovereign, free and independent; to all who shall see these presents, greeting:

Whereas, in and by our commission, dated at Philadelphia, the 30th day of September, in the year of our Lord one thousand seven hundred and seventy six, Benjamin Franklin, one of the delegates in Congress from the state of

Pennsylvania, and president of the convention of the said State, &c. Silas Deane, late a delegate from the State of Connecticut, and Arthur Lee, barrister at law, were nominated and appointed our commissioners, with full powers to treat, agree, and conclude with his most Christian majesty the king of France, or with such person or persons as should be by him for that purpose authorized, of and upon a true and sincere friendship, and a firm, inviolable, and universal peace, for the defence, protection, and safety of the navigation and mutual commerce of the subjects of his most Christian majesty and the people of the United States, we, promising in good faith to ratify whatsoever our said commissioners should transact in the premises; and, whereas, our said commissioners, in pursuance of their full powers, on the 6th day of February last, at Paris, with Conrad Alexander Gérard, royal syndic of the city of Strasburg, secretary of his most Christian majesty's council of state, by virtue of powers plenipotentiary to him granted by his most Christian majesty, and dated the 30th day of January, in the year of our Lord one thousand seven hundred and seventy eight, did conclude and sign, on the part of the crown of France, and of the United States of America, a (treaty of amity and commerce, or treaty of alliance, or act separate and secret) in the following words, (here insert the respective treaties verbatim, French and English).

Now know ye, that we, the said Congress, have unanimously ratified and confirmed, and by these presents do ratify and confirm the said treaty, and every part, article, and clause thereof, on our part concluded and signed as aforesaid; and further do authorize and direct our commissioners at the court of France, or any of them, to deliver this our act of ratification in exchange for the ratification of the said treaty on the part of his most Christian majesty the king of France and Navarre.

Done in Congress at York town, in the state of Pennsylvania, this 4th day of May, in the year of our Lord one thousand seven hundred and seventy eight.

In testimony whereof, the President, by order of the said Congress, hath hereunto subscribed his name and affixed his seal.

Attest. *President,* (L. S.)

Secretary.

Ordered, That six copies of the treaties, with the ratification agreed to, be made out and transmitted by the Committee for Foreign Affairs to the commissioners of the United States at the court of France, by different conveyances.

Ordered, That the Marine Committee provide vessels for said despatches.

Ordered, That the committee appointed to prepare the form of ratification, &c. be directed to prepare a proper publication on the present occasion.

WEDNESDAY, MAY 6, 1778

. . . .

The committee appointed to prepare a publication, brought in a draught which was read, and after debate,

Resolved, That the same be re-committed.

That Mr. G[ouverneur] Morris be added to the said committee.

THREE O'CLOCK, P. M.

The committee to whom was re-committed the draught for publication, brought in another draught, which was taken into consideration, and agreed to as follows:

Whereas, Congress have received from their commissioners at the court of France, copies of a treaty of amity

and commerce, and of a treaty of alliance, between the crown of France and these United States, duly entered into and executed at Paris, on the 6th day of February last, by a minister properly authorized by his most Christian majesty on the one part, and the said commissioners on the other part: and whereas, the said treaties have been maturely considered and unanimously ratified and confirmed by Congress;

It is recommended to the Inhabitants of these United States, that they regard and treat the subjects of France as those of a magnanimous and generous Ally. For it is with pleasure that Congress inform the Public that his most Christian Majesty, declining to avail himself of the situation of these United States, engaged in a war with a powerful and cruel Enemy, hath with a magnanimity becoming a great Prince, generously treated on terms of perfect equality and mutual benefit. And to the end that all proper alacrity may be shewn in giving aid and protection to the commerce, property and persons, of the subjects of his Most Christian Majesty, the following extracts from said Treaties are published for the information of all, and for regulating the conduct of those whom it may more immediately concern.[1]

in which said treaty of amity and commerce are the articles following, to wit: (here insert Art. 6, 7, 14, 15, 16, 17, 20, 21, 25, 26, 27, and 29, with the form of the passports.) Now, therefore, to the end, that the said treaty may be well and faithfully performed and kept on the part and behalf of these United States:

Resolved, That all captains, commanders, and other officers and seamen belonging to any of the vessels of war of these United States, or any of them, or of any private armed vessels commissioned by Congress, and all other the subjects of these United States, do govern themselves strictly in all things according to the above recited articles; and that they do afford the same aid and protection to the per-

[1] To this point the report, in the writing of Francis Dana, is in the *Papers of the Continental Congress,* No. 29, folio 303. What follows is based upon rough notes in the writing of Gouverneur Morris, on folio 301. W. C. F.

sons, commerce and property of the subjects of his most Christian majesty, as is due to the persons, commerce and property of the inhabitants of these United States;

And further it is recommended to all the inhabitants of these states to consider the subjects of his most Christian majesty as their brethren and allies, and that they behave towards them with the friendship and attention due to the subjects of a great prince, who, with the highest magnanimity and wisdom hath treated with these United States on terms of perfect equality and mutual advantage, thereby rendering himself the protector of the rights of mankind.

Resolved, That a committee of three be appointed to prepare an address to the inhabitants of these states, upon the present situation of public affairs:

The members chosen, Mr. R[ichard] H[enry] Lee, Mr. [Samuel] Chase and Mr. [Gouverneur] Morris.